WALKING THE OLD WAYS OF HEREFORDSHIRE

~ FULLY UPDATED AND REVISED ~

WALKING THE OLD WAYS OF HEREFORDSHIRE

The history in the landscape explored through 52 circular walks

Andy & Karen Johnson

LOGASTON PRESS

LOGASTON PRESS
The Holme, Church Road, Eardisley, Herefordshire HR3 6NJ
An imprint of Fircone Books Ltd.
www.logastonpress.co.uk

First published by Logaston Press September 2014
Reprinted May 2016, May 2018, July 2019
Revised edition February 2022

ISBN 978-1-906663-86-5

Typeset by Logaston Press. Printed and bound in Poland

Logaston Press is committed to a sustainable future for our business, our readers and our planet.
This book is made from paper certified by the Forest Stewardship Council

British Library Catalogue in Publishing Data
A CIP catalogue record for this book is available from the British Library

THE WHETSTONE

This stone is a glacial erratic, a stone carried by a glacier and set down when the glacier retreated. Local folklore has it that the stone goes to the brook below every morning that it hears a cock crow. Be that as it may, when there was an outbreak of plague in Kington, a market was instead held at the stone where wheat was sold, hence the name 'whet'. Another derivation of the name would imply that the stone was used for sharpening knives and other implements.

MONKEY PUZZLES

The monkey puzzles on Hergest Ridge are certainly a bit of a puzzle. One theory is that they were planted by the Banks family of Hergest Croft as a landmark to commemorate Sir Joseph Banks, the naturalist who accompanied Captain Cook on his voyage in the *Endeavour* down the coast of South America (where the monkey puzzle tree has its native home) and thence into the Pacific. However, Sir Joseph Banks died childless and according to Elizabeth Banks, he only *might* be related to her husband Lawrence. (Elizabeth and Lawrence Banks are the current owners of Hergest Croft, see p.9.) One story indicates that the trees were planted in the Victorian period, and Lawrence Banks has stated that they were planted by his father as a riposte to another group that he could see on another nearby hillside; but if this second group did exist decades ago, they certainly aren't visible now.

6 Drop down from the Whetstone onto the race-course and turn right. Walk along this to pick up the path from the monkey puzzles on which you turn left to head gently down the spine of Hergest Ridge, in due course reaching a gate that leads onto a tarmacked lane that carries on down the spine towards Kington.

7 At the start of the tarmacked lane, part of the arboretum of Hergest Croft gardens is on your right, and you may want to take the signposted footpath off to the right that you soon reach, to take a short stroll into, and then back out of, the collection of azaleas, birches and other plants and trees gathered together here. Follow the lane down to the main road at the bottom, where you turn right and then left on a lane from which you enter the churchyard.

HERGEST CROFT GARDENS

Hergest Croft Gardens include an old fashioned kitchen garden, an azalea garden, a maple grove and Park Wood, through whose rhododendrons this walk passes. The gardens have been in the ownership of the Banks family since 1814. Some of the earliest exotic trees and the now huge Douglas firs in Yeld Wood were planted in the later 1800s, but it was in the early 1900s that the gardens started to take their current shape, especially with the acquisition of the Hergest Estate. The gardens fell into decline during the Second World War, but restoration begun in 1953 under Richard and Jane Banks, who also began to plant what have become national collections of maples and birches. Lawrence Banks and his wife, Elizabeth, have managed the gardens since 1988. The gardens tend to be open daily in the afternoon between the end of March and the beginning of November, and at weekends in March, but check www.hergest.co.uk or 01544 230160.

KNILL COURT & CHURCH

Knill Court, which lies due south of the church by the Hindwell Brook, is hidden by trees for most of the walk, though the building can be seen as one descends Rushock Hill. The date of the original house is unclear. Parts may have dated to the 14th century, and records suggest that it was enlarged in 1561. One of the owners of Knill Court was Samuel Romilly, the son of French Protestant emigrés, who became a lawyer and politician. He married Anne Garbett, the daughter of Francis Garbett of Knill, who was secretary to Lord Lansdowne. Romilly was a man of great probity, but suffered from stress and in 1818, shortly after Anne died, he cut his throat.

Knill Court was the home of Sir John Walsh from 1839, and it was he who extensively modernised it in the 1840s. Walsh became the Conservative MP for the Radnorshire County seat in 1841, an election that cost him £4,000, and he was unopposed in the succeeding elections of 1847, 1852, 1857, 1859 and 1865. (Historians believe that there was an informal non-aggression pact that gave the Tories the County seat, and the Liberals the Radnorshire Boroughs seat, though elections were sometimes contested, as the County seat was in 1841.) Walsh increased the size of his estate, from about 6,000 acres in 1833 to nearly 12,500 acres in 1873, which in those days also meant he could control more votes. The house was modernised in 1867 to the design of George Shrimpton, and the gardens redesigned with 'pleasure grounds' and a walled garden, together with a small park. A sale catalogue of c.1900 shows that the Court had been separated from the surrounding estate, but retained 6 acres of pleasure grounds, three tennis lawns, an Italian garden, rhododendrons, two kitchen gardens, a forcing house, gardener's cottage and potting sheds. The house was destroyed in a fire in 1943 when in use as a girls' boarding school, and the gardens abandoned. A later house was built on part of the site.

The church dates from the late 12th or early 13th century, and contains a fine 13th-century font with carvings on the panels surrounding the bowl. In the church you will also see a plaque with the following words: 'To the glory of God and in thanksgiving to Him for the victory granted to us in the Great War of 1914-1918 and for His mercies in bringing safely home the men of this parish who served their country overseas.' In other words, Knill was one of the 53 settlements in England and Wales known as 'thankful' because none of their men was killed in the First World War.

where the track on your right passes close to the fenced corner of the field on your left. There's a view to the left and behind you of the Clee Hills. From this point don't follow the track (which heads towards a copse of conifers), but bear half-left from it, aiming for a point on the edge of the field about 500 yards to the left of the conifer copse. As you cross the field, you should eventually spot, and head for, an Offa's Dyke Path fingerpost jutting above the fenceline. Once you reach this post, you will be following the Offa's Dyke Path.

5 Turn right along the path signposted 'Lower Harpton'. It initially leads along the line of the obvious Dyke, which presently bends to the left and starts to head downhill. You eventually leave a landscape of fields and head into bracken-rich moorland. After a couple of hundred yards the path departs from the ancient Dyke.

13

OFFA'S DYKE

'There was in Mercia in fairly recent times a certain vigorous king called Offa, who terrified all the neighbouring kings and provinces around him, and who had a great dyke built between Wales and Mercia from sea to sea.' So wrote Asser in his *Life of King Alfred* in 893, nearly a hundred years after the Dyke's construction. The comment 'from sea to sea' has bedevilled the Dyke ever since. Presuming the 'seas' to be the north Welsh coast and the Severn Estuary, antiquarians, historians and map makers have linked various dykes together and called the whole 'Offa's Dyke'. But the Dyke can only securely be said to run from near the north Welsh coast to near Kington, and probably to the Wye to the north-west of Hereford. There is no evidence of any dyke that could form part of a 'sea to sea' structure over a 20-mile stretch in the vicinity of Hereford, and whilst there are a number of dykes further south, it is difficult to be certain that they once formed part of a continuous structure.

Even the part which can be safely called Offa's Dyke because of a certain uniformity in its form and route across the landscape varies in its structure depending upon the type of soil, the lie of the land and, presumably, the numbers of workmen, their commitment and the skill of the foreman. Originally the V-shaped ditch to the west was cut about 2 metres deep, and the bank raised some 8 metres above the bottom of the ditch. Sometimes there is a small bank on the outer side of the ditch, but this may simply have been created when clearing out debris from the ditch once the Dyke had been constructed rather than being part of the design. The ground was first stripped of its turves, which were placed in the bank as it was constructed to help hold the loose soil together. Turves were also taken from behind the Dyke, sometimes creating the false impression that a ditch was also dug on the east of the Dyke. No evidence for any palisade on the Dyke has been found, nor 'gateways' through it, the current gaps being modern creations or those left for streams and rivers. Underneath the Dyke have been found small marking out trenches and the occasional post hole, presumably where a stake was hammered into the ground to mark the line of the Dyke.

What was the Dyke's purpose? The evidence of the structure to the north of Kington suggests it was meant as a boundary marker between the kingdom of Mercia as it was in the 790s, and that of Powys, and it is certainly an impressive structure when viewed from the Welsh side, when the careful choice of its position on hillslopes is clear to see. It was never constructed to be a defendable line like Hadrian's Wall, but it could have been patrolled to keep an eye out for Welsh raiding parties, and its steep bank and ditch would have hindered rustlers marching away with oxen, cattle and sheep. Yet there is no evidence that the Dyke was ever maintained; the ditch would have started to fill in from the day it was completed. Perhaps its real purpose lies in Offa's attempt to equate himself with the greatest king of his age, Charlemagne. In or shortly before 789, Charlemagne suggested that one of Offa's daughters marry his eldest son, to which Offa responded that that would be acceptable if his own son, Ecgfrith, could marry one of Charlemagne's daughters. This so irked Charlemagne that he closed Frankish ports to English merchants. Could it be that Offa, in his own fit of pique and rage (his character suggests he was capable of both) decided on a project that would mark him out as an equal of Charlemagne, and that this project was the building of Britain's greatest Dyke?

6 Turn right to cross Herrock Hill Common and the saddle in the hills, still following the Offa's Dyke Path, and then bear half-left to slant down and across the hillside back towards Lower Harpton Farm. It crosses a stile part way down the hillside (there's a view down to Knill Court), and later swings left past a couple of cottages. As it nears Lower Harpton Farm, the path goes through a small gate on the right of the track, crosses a field to a gate near the farm buildings and so onto a track that leads down to the road (the B4362).

7 Just before the road, look out for a footpath sign on the right and cross a stile into a field. Follow the waymarked path alongside the field boundary on your left, which soon also encompasses a stream. Keep following this stream, crossing three field boundaries.

8 As you start to approach the settlement of Knill, turn left (opposite a stand of oak trees) to re-cross the Hindwell Brook via a footbridge reached just after a vehicular bridge and track. Once across the bridge, initially follow the boundaries of the house on your right, passing through a gateway, then heading across to the next 'outer' corner of the property's boundary from where you pick up the line of an old track on up the hillside on much the same line and departing from the property's boundary, to pass through a gateway near the crest of the rise. At this point the line of the path turns slightly to the left, to head across the field you're in and leave it by a gate onto a tarmacked lane. Turn right along the lane, and shortly you will come to the church drive where you parked your car.

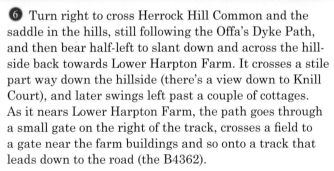

Walk 3
Lyonshall
& Titley Junction

4 miles, largely on minor roads, woodland paths and field edge paths. One stile. Includes an old railway line, restored station and rolling stock, a castle site on private ground with some surviving stone-work, and a church.

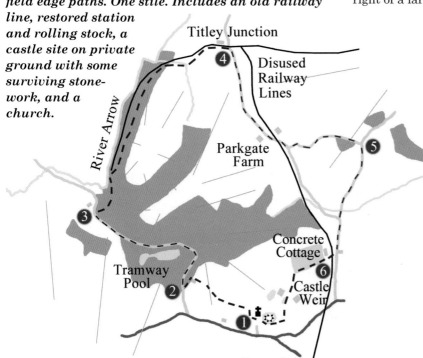

Park in the car park by Lyonshall church (GR 331 563).

1 Take the footpath that starts from the top corner of the car park furthest from the church. Go through the gate and turn right along the hedgeline. Within tens of yards go through another gate and then turn half-left to diagonally cross the next field to its far corner, passing just to the right of a large oak that stands alone in the field. Go through the gate here and walk along the field boundary on your right to another gate on the far side of the field (passing gates to your right). Go through the gate and again follow the field boundary on your right to a further gate.

Through this gate follow the fence on your right and you will soon find yourself facing a small footpath gate that leads to a path fenced on both sides: go through the gate and follow this path which will lead you at its end to another small gate into a field. Go through the gate and turn left to follow the field boundary on your left, passing round the second of two houses as you join a track to leave the field. Walk down this track to a minor road.

2 Turn right on the road and follow this along above Tramway Pool, which you soon reach in the woodland on your left. In due course the woods give way to a field on your left.

3 As you near the end of this field, and before you reach a cottage on the left-hand side of the road, take the bridleway off to the right into the woodland. This path is part of the Herefordshire Way, a route that circuits the county close to the county boundary. Keep on this path: it will lead you down close to the river Arrow, then back uphill to shadow part of the old railway line between Kington and Leominster, on which some rolling stock might be stationed. Track has been relaid here and forms part of the modern set up of Titley Junction. The path shadows the railway line for a while, before leaving the wood. At this point keep to the left-hand edge of the field, passing a railway bridge (see photo opposite) to cross a stream at a point about 100 yards up from the railway bridge and enter the next field.

Cross this field to a gate just to the right of a green Dutch barn, around which is parked and piled much of the railway and other paraphernalia that is now Titley Junction. Keep to the path beyond this gate and it will lead you past the old Titley Junction station buildings (now a private house) and so out onto a road.

TITLEY JUNCTION

Titley Junction was where four lines of the Great Western Railway met: one from Presteigne to the north, another from Leominster to the east, a third from Hay and Eardisley to the south, and the fourth from New Radnor and Kington to the west. At its height of activity the junction would have seen some 30 trains a day, but passenger traffic to Hay and Eardisley ceased in 1940 and on the other lines in the early '50s. Freight trains continued to run from Leominster to Presteigne till 1961 and to Kington till 1964, after which the lines were dismantled. The restoration of the station and goods yard began in the 1980s, and under new owners since 2001 the line has been restored westwards towards Bullocks Mill.

④ Turn right on the road, and follow it past the collection of buildings that is Parkgate Farm and turn left on the minor road just past the entrance to Hollybush Farm. (You could carry straight on here, turning right when you reach a T-junction, but this slightly longer route is on quieter roads and has a pleasant grassy avenue for part of its length.) Follow this road till it ends at a T-junction.

⑤ Turn right here and follow the road, passing another road junction on your right, until you come to a house on the left-hand side of the road. (At this point the two routes will have rejoined.) Take the path to the right opposite this house, which begins its life as a driveway and passes under a bridge that carried the railway line from Eardisley and Almeley to Titley Junction. Once under the bridge, keep to the left-hand side of the parking area by the aptly-named Concrete Cottage and walk up some steps to a gate into the orchard behind the cottage.

⑥ Walk uphill following the boundary on your left. At the top corner of the orchard pass out onto a track on which you turn left. Follow this track which presently gains a tarmacked surface. Pass alongside a tall stone wall on your left, beyond which you'll come to the entrance gates to Castle Weir. Opposite these, cross the stile on the right-hand side of the lane and take the footpath which slants up to the edge of some wooded ground,

LYONSHALL CHURCH
The church dates mainly from the late 13th and early 14th centuries, with traces of earlier Norman work, and has what has been termed an 'elegant and unusual' north arcade in the Early English style.

passing through a gate to enter this wood just short of the church. If you want to glance at the castle, go up the bank on the right, but to return to your car, keep ahead to another gate to reach the churchyard.

LYONSHALL CASTLE

The castle covers an extensive area. The inner bailey, on which stand sections of curtain wall and the remains of a circular keep, probably built in the late 1100s or early 1200s, is surrounded by a moat. Traces of window openings and a doorway can be seen in the remaining stonework. The keep was probably approached by a stairway on its southern side as there were traces of this still visible in the 1870s. There is a well in the eastern part of the inner bailey. An outer bailey extends slightly to the south, but mainly to the north-east, towards the modern farm buildings, with embankments still visible. The modern farm buildings themselves sit on further earthworks.

The castle is not mentioned in the Domesday Survey and was probably established soon afterwards by the de Lacy family, passing from them to the Devereuxs and then the de Vere family. Orders were issued for its defence in April 1264, a time of tension and warfare between Prince Llewelyn, Simon de Montfort and Prince Edward (later Edward I). During Edward's reign the castle was held by William Touchet, who gained a licence for a weekly market and Michaelmas fair, this was at a time when Lyonshall had borough status. In the 1380s the castle was briefly held by Sir Simon Burley, appointed tutor to the future Richard II by Richard's father, Edward the Black Prince. But after the Black Prince's death and Richard's coronation, Simon de Burley became *persona non grata* to the group of barons known as the Lords Appellant, and he was executed. In 1391 a contract between Sir John Devereux and John Brown, a mason of Hereford, describes a new stone hall that was to measure 44 feet long by 26 feet wide. At the same time, the gatehouse was to be enlarged and repaired and a portcullis provided, together with quarters for a guard. Presumably some of this work was carried out and the castle was in a reasonable state of repair early the following century, for in 1404 it was ordered to be fortified against Owain Glyndwr. The castle probably fell into disuse relatively soon afterwards.

NEWPORT HOUSE

A medieval house once stood here (which might have been home to Sir John Oldcastle, see p.26), but was demolished and replaced with the present building between 1712 and 1718, following the purchase of the estate by the Foley family of Great Witley, who had made their fortune in the iron industry. In 1860 it was acquired by the grandson of the engineer James Watt, who extended the house, including adding a large reception hall lit by a stained glass lantern in the roof, and employed W.A. Nesfield to redesign the garden. The house was bought by Herefordshire Council in 1919 for use as an isolation TB hospital, and then in 1953 it became a home for Latvians who had become refugees after their country was occupied first by Nazi Germany in the Second World War and then by Soviet Russia during the Cold War. In 1996 the council sold the property, and it has since passed through two owners until acquired by recent owners who carried out extensive renovation work to the house and the gardens – formal, walled and parkland.

❷ Cross the road and go through the gate into a field. The path across this field passes about 10 yards to the right of the nearest oak that stands in the field. As you pass this tree, your target becomes a corner of hedgerow that juts into the field. When you reach this, turn slightly left to follow the hedgerow now on your left towards a little paddock that lies to the left of a white-painted house. At the end of the field, cross into the paddock then

LYONSHALL CASTLE

The castle covers an extensive area. The inner bailey, on which stand sections of curtain wall and the remains of a circular keep, probably built in the late 1100s or early 1200s, is surrounded by a moat. Traces of window openings and a doorway can be seen in the remaining stonework. The keep was probably approached by a stairway on its southern side as there were traces of this still visible in the 1870s. There is a well in the eastern part of the inner bailey. An outer bailey extends slightly to the south, but mainly to the north-east, towards the modern farm buildings, with embankments still visible. The modern farm buildings themselves sit on further earthworks.

The castle is not mentioned in the Domesday Survey and was probably established soon afterwards by the de Lacy family, passing from them to the Devereuxs and then the de Vere family. Orders were issued for its defence in April 1264, a time of tension and warfare between Prince Llewelyn, Simon de Montfort and Prince Edward (later Edward I). During Edward's reign the castle was held by William Touchet, who gained a licence for a weekly market and Michaelmas fair, this was at a time when Lyonshall had borough status. In the 1380s the castle was briefly held by Sir Simon Burley, appointed tutor to the future Richard II by Richard's father, Edward the Black Prince. But after the Black Prince's death and Richard's coronation, Simon de Burley became *persona non grata* to the group of barons known as the Lords Appellant, and he was executed. In 1391 a contract between Sir John Devereux and John Brown, a mason of Hereford, describes a new stone hall that was to measure 44 feet long by 26 feet wide. At the same time, the gatehouse was to be enlarged and repaired and a portcullis provided, together with quarters for a guard. Presumably some of this work was carried out and the castle was in a reasonable state of repair early the following century, for in 1404 it was ordered to be fortified against Owain Glyndwr. The castle probably fell into disuse relatively soon afterwards.

Walk 4
Almeley

3 miles, largely on paths crossing fields, woodland tracks and minor roads. Several stiles. Includes a church, two castle mottes (or 'twts'), and a Quaker meeting house, and passes round the gardens of Newport House and its restored walled vegetable garden.

Park near the church (see p.28) (GR 333 515).

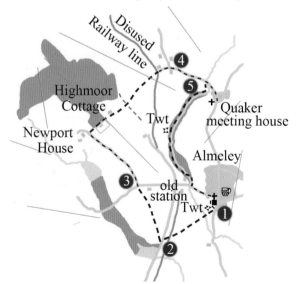

❶ In the churchyard, with your back to the church entrance, turn left along the path and leave the churchyard. Turn right and immediately right again to cross a stile into the field adjacent to the churchyard. From this point your path leads to the left of the castle mound and the remains of the medieval fishponds beyond to cross a stream in the valley bottom by a bridge. Across the bridge, keep to the right of a group of trees and a telegraph pole to cross this field. Look to your right to see the stone building which was Almeley's railway station. At the far side, cross the bridge and stile and then cross the next field on much the same line and go over another stile into an orchard. Cross a corner of the orchard, keeping on the same line, to the far side where a gate leads you out onto a road.

ALMELEY STATION

The Kington and Eardisley Railway Company, formed in 1862, built its line in part on the route of the old horse-drawn tramway that ran from Eardisley to Kington. Work commenced on the line the following year, but the company was soon bankrupt. Construction was begun again in 1872 by the Leominster & Kington Railway and the line opened in August 1874. The facilities at Almeley were notoriously sparse, with no accommodation for the stationmaster and no signal boxes. The line was taken over by the Great Western Railway Company in 1897 and closed between 1917 and 1922. Almeley station was closed for good in 1940 and the line itself in 1962.

ALMELEY TWT

The photo shows the twt on the right and Almeley Manor on the skyline. The name twt, pronounced 'toot', comes from the Anglo-Saxon for a lookout. The 20-feet high motte near the church is the remains of a castle probably built during the reign of King John on the site of an earlier structure that might have been built in the times of the Anarchy, the wars between Stephen and Matilda. Henry III visited it in 1231 when en route from his new castle at Painscastle to Hereford and is said to have received the homage here of Simon de Montfort, when Simon was seeking the restoration of the lands of the earldom of Leicester. Stonework is said to have been exposed on the south side of the motte when a tree fell some years ago, and the motte is thought to have supported a round or polygonal stone tower. A bailey existed to the north-west, but part of this now lies under the churchyard. A possible further bailey extended to the south-east. To the south-west, in the valley bottom, are the earth-work remains of two rectangular fishponds which would have been used to supply fish to the occupants of the castle.

NEWPORT HOUSE

A medieval house once stood here (which might have been home to Sir John Oldcastle, see p.26), but was demolished and replaced with the present building between 1712 and 1718, following the purchase of the estate by the Foley family of Great Witley, who had made their fortune in the iron industry. In 1860 it was acquired by the grandson of the engineer James Watt, who extended the house, including adding a large reception hall lit by a stained glass lantern in the roof, and employed W.A. Nesfield to redesign the garden. The house was bought by Herefordshire Council in 1919 for use as an isolation TB hospital, and then in 1953 it became a home for Latvians who had become refugees after their country was occupied first by Nazi Germany in the Second World War and then by Soviet Russia during the Cold War. In 1996 the council sold the property, and it has since passed through two owners until acquired by recent owners who carried out extensive renovation work to the house and the gardens – formal, walled and parkland.

❷ Cross the road and go through the gate into a field. The path across this field passes about 10 yards to the right of the nearest oak that stands in the field. As you pass this tree, your target becomes a corner of hedgerow that juts into the field. When you reach this, turn slightly left to follow the hedgerow now on your left towards a little paddock that lies to the left of a white-painted house. At the end of the field, cross into the paddock then

ALMELEY QUAKER MEETING HOUSE
The building dates from 1672 and is one of the oldest
continually used Quaker meeting houses in the country.
Two of the early members of the meeting, Edward Prichard
and John Eckley, were involved with William Penn in setting
up the colony of Pennsylvania in 1682.

continue to follow the hedge on your left to a stile on the
far side which you cross to reach a road.

3 Cross the road and walk up the lane that services
Newport House. At the crossroads between the house and
the walled garden, turn right and follow the track past
the walled garden on your immediate right. Pass to the
right of Highmoor Cottage and go through a gate, then
keep the hedge to your right and walk along the field edge
and out through a gate at the far end. Cross the track and
go through the gate on the other side into a field. Aim for
the far top left of the field and leave it through a metal
gate (the right-hand one of the two gates in that corner of
the field). Follow the hedge to your left and go through a
gateway to cross a stream. Climb the bank then turn left
along the footpath to reach a footpath gate. Go through
the gate and you'll find yourself on a lane.

4 Turn right, and immediately look right to see the
route of the old railway. Follow the lane to a T-junction,
turn right and follow this lane along to another

BATCH OR OLDCASTLE TWT

Batch Twt is located at the end of a spur of ground that slopes steeply down to two streams. Its remains consist of a small motte and a bailey to the north, where a modern cottage may now sit on top of the old entrance. There are faint indications that the castle lies above a Roman site, which might explain why the family who lived here in the 1300s had the name Oldcastle. Indeed, the site is said to be the birthplace of Sir John Oldcastle. Sir John was one of the commanders of the forces under the overall command of Prince Henry (the future Henry V) in the wars against Owain Glyndwr, towards the end of which he married into the aristocracy and became Lord Cobham. As such, Oldcastle was one of the commanders of an expeditionary force sent to France in 1411 that was to lay the ground for Henry V's intervention in France. However, Oldcastle held Lollard beliefs that challenged the practice and bureaucracy of the established Church and when Henry ascended the throne, he had to sacrifice Oldcastle to gain Church support for his French venture. Oldcastle was condemned as a heretic and imprisoned in the Tower of London, from where he escaped and led an ill-planned and abortive Lollard revolt. He managed to avoid capture and fled to the borders of England and Wales, where he lived in hiding till he was caught in 1417, and hung as a traitor and burnt as a heretic. Shakespeare wrote a character he called Oldcastle into his plays of *Henry IV*, but a subsequent Lord Cobham (of whom Oldcastle was the stepfather of his great-great-great-grandmother) became Elizabeth I's Lord Chamberlain. Fearing taint as a traitor, Cobham forced Shakespeare to change Oldcastle's name, which he did – to Falstaff.

T-junction, to the right of which is Almeley Quaker Meeting House. Having visited this, go back to the T-junction and return down the lane you walked up, passing a junction with another road.

5 Then, take the track that forks off to the left (opposite a white-painted house). The track will lead you past a few houses above a stream. When the track starts to climb uphill, take the path that forks left, keeping close to the stream. Soon you'll pass the second Almeley Twt. The path twice crosses the stream, and shortly after the second crossing joins a driveway. Walk down this to the road ahead, and turn left to return to the church.

ALMELEY CHURCH

The tower dates from around 1200, whilst the rest of the church dates to the Decorated period. The church's unusual feature is a painted ceilure, that part of the nave roof adjacent to the chancel which would have been above the former rood, a cross bearing Christ's body and usually flanked by carvings of the Virgin Mary and John the Baptist supported on a beam. The incorporation of Tudor roses in the design dates it to the early 16th century. A Jacobean screen has been re-sited under the tower arch.

Walk 5
Pembridge

3.25 miles, largely on paths crossing or along the edge of fields, minor roads and tracks. Includes one of Herefordshire's Black and White Villages, a disused railway line, the enigmatic Rowe Ditch and a church.

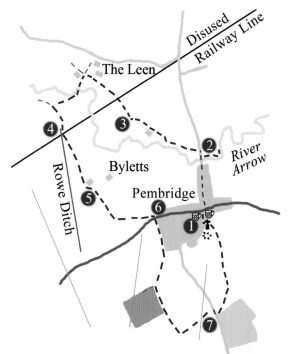

Park near the Market Hall/New Inn (GR 390 531).

1 With your back to the Market Hall and the New Inn on your left, walk down to the main road, on which you turn right and then immediately left (opposite the Olde Steppes shop and café), and walk down the road sign-posted to Presteigne and Shobdon. Cross the bridge over the river Arrow.

Here you may want to explore the Village Green Conservation Area on the right. The parish council implemented a management plan in 2008 which aimed to transform an area of ungrazed grassland into a mixture of species-rich hay meadow and wet woodland. Information boards at the entrance to the Green tell you more.

NEW INN

Known as Cooke's Public House in 1804, much of the building is of early 17th-century date, notably the western wing and that erected at the rear of the premises. There used to be dormer windows in the roof that probably provided light to the servants' rooms.

MARKET HALL

This dates to the early 16th century and would originally have had a first-floor room, serving the needs of what was then a medieval borough with a population of some 2,000 people. One of the pillars that support the current roof sits on the socket stone of a 14th-century cross that once stood here. Near another pillar, just outside the hall, there once stood a squarish stone standing about 18 inches high which Alfred Watkins believed to be a mark stone on a ley line. The village stocks used to be kept here.

DUPPA'S ALMSHOUSES

These were founded in 1661 by Jeffrey Duppa to house six elderly folk, a foundation augmented by his son Bryan Duppa, bishop of Winchester. They were altered in the late 19th century and again in the 20th, and now comprise just four houses.

2 The walk continues by crossing the road at the entrance to the village green and taking the gravelled track that leads across a parking area and then towards a farm. Go through a gate across the track and just after the end of the open ground on the right the path turns right through a newly installed gate. Follow the line of the field boundary on your right and so pass to the right of all the farm buildings, via a couple of gates, then keep following the fence across a small field to a stile.

3 Cross the stile and turn right along the track, which passes The Leen farm on your right and then meets another track at a 'crossroads'. Turn left here to pass three houses on your right, and follow the track across the river Arrow. At the split in the track just beyond the river crossing, take the right-hand fork and follow it to the end of the next field. Here, turn left in front of the hedgerow,

and follow this down to a stile at the far end of the field, crossing over this onto a disused railway track.

RAILWAY LINE

The railway line was a single track line between Leominster and Kington opened on 28 July 1857. Intermediate stations were at Kingsland, Pembridge and Titley together with 'halts' at Marston and the Ox House in Shobdon, the latter for the use of Lord Bateman of Shobdon Court, the chairman of the company that built the line. The line was subsequently extended to New Radnor, with branch lines to Eardisley and Presteigne. The Great Western Railway took over the line in 1898. During the Second World War the line was used for hospital trains carrying up to 300 wounded soldiers each to the two American hospitals outside Kington. The last passenger train ran in 1955, and the last goods train in 1964, when the line was closed.

4 Cross the railway line to another two stiles and enter the field on the far side of the line. The bank and ditch on your immediate right is the Rowe Ditch.

THE ROWE DITCH

This 'ditch' is a cross valley dyke, with a ditch on its western side, erected by English settlers to help deter their Celtic neighbours from stock rustling and other raids. Such dykes are not uncommon, but this is one of the larger ones, its remaining length being two miles though originally it was even longer. Excavations in 2003 showed that cropmarks revealed by aerial photography as straddling the line of the ditch belong to a site occupied in the Iron Age and Roman period, probably as a farmstead, thus confirming the Rowe Ditch's later origins, probably in the 7th century. Excavations in the 1970s and '80s elsewhere along the line of the ditch show that it was up to 2m deep and 5m wide.

The path diverges slightly from the Rowe Ditch. Aim roughly for the first telegraph pole into the field from the line of the Ditch, and walk towards a gate and stile on the far side of the field. Cross the stile and then walk up the field boundary on your left, leaving the field in the top left-hand corner by a field gate near a house.

5 Turn right here onto the lane that leads away from the house (with The Byletts further along the lane), cross the stream in the valley bottom, then, after a further 70

THE BYLETTS

The core of this building is an Elizabethan mansion rich in oak beams and panelling. The family who owned it suffered financial losses through their support for the king in the Civil War, and the house gradually deteriorated until it came into the ownership of S. Bowle Evans, who remodelled it in 1879. It is now divided into flats. The grounds used to contain a walled garden, a pigeon house and a pond.

yards or so, pass through the kissing gate on the left and walk diagonally up and across the field to its far right-hand corner.

6 Leave the field by another kissing gate and take the track signposted by a public footpath sign almost opposite on the far side of the road. This leads just to the left of a red-brick house, then to the right of a series of 1960s and later houses, before passing between fields to left and right and then starting to turn slightly to the right. Just past a tumbledown barn on the left you reach a plantation of poplars, and here you turn left up the slope, keeping the poplar plantation on your immediate right. Go through the kissing gate at the top, and then follow the field boundary on your right alongside the next field. At the top of this field pass through the hedge into the next field and turn left to follow the field boundary. At the far end of the field go through the kissing gate onto a road.

7 Turn right on the road, and after 60 yards or so, take the footpath gate on your left into a field. The path you want diagonally crosses the field to reach a footpath gate, but it might be easier to follow the field boundaries

on your right around two sides of the field to its far corner. Go through the gate and turn half-left, aiming just to the right of the church. (In summer the church may be hidden behind trees ... in that case, head for an oak in the hedgeline, halfway between two telegraph poles. It's also possible that the path may be obstructed by crops, in which case follow the permissive headland path to the left until you reach the oak tree mentioned above.) To the left of the oak go through a gate into another field. Follow the field boundary on your left to a kissing gate through which you enter the churchyard, noticing the site of Pembridge Castle to your left. To return to the Market Hall, keep the church on your left and follow a tarmac path from near the bell tower.

PEMBRIDGE CASTLE

A castle on a site to the immediate south-west of the churchyard is first mentioned in 1219. Stone found on the mound, and its presence in the later buildings, indicates that a stone-built structure once stood on the mound. Silas Taylor, the antiquary and Parliamentary officer in the Civil War who helped John Birch when the latter was governor of Hereford and later was known to Samuel Pepys, visited Pembridge in the mid 17th century and wrote of a 'mansion house where there are as yet the remains of a fortified keep or small castle'. Excavations in 2004 found the foundations of 11th-century stone walls, and also evidence that the castle had been destroyed and rebuilt at least once.

PEMBRIDGE CHURCH

Most of the existing structure was built in the 14th century in what was then the new Decorated style, with curvilinear tracery in many of the windows. The font is 13th-century and the pulpit Jacobean (look for the carvings of monsters). In the chancel are the tombs of probable members of the Gour family who lived at Marston, a hamlet a few miles away. One pair is shown as a knight and his lady, the other pair unusually in civilian attire. The west door of the church is original and bears the marks of bullets fired during a skirmish during the later stages of the first Civil War as the Royalists gradually lost control of the county to Parliamentary forces. The separate bell-tower hides a remarkable four post timber structure that carries the bells, dated to a period between 1207 and 1216, although it was probably rebuilt in the 1670s. The thick stone wall at ground level with narrow windows was almost certainly built as a refuge for the townsfolk. (Herefordshire once had nine bell towers standing detached from their church, most of which were so constructed as refuges for the local population in times of strife.) To see the interior of the tower, insert the relevant coin in the electricity meter just inside the door.

Walk 6
Shobdon, Kingsland & Mortimers Cross

9.5 miles, largely on field-edge paths and minor roads. A few stiles. Includes two churches, two castle sites, Kingsland village, an SSSI, the site of the Battle of Mortimers Cross, and drumlins.

Park near the church at Shobdon (GR 621 408).

1 You may want to begin the walk by visiting the Shobdon Arches at the top of the wide grassy avenue of mature trees. Then, walk back down from the Arches and continue ahead, with the church (for which see overleaf) on your left. Pass the stables of Shobdon Court (now converted into housing) and a walled garden. Just past a lake on your right, go through a footpath gate on the left.

2 Follow the path down towards the lake ahead, before swinging gently left to pass between this lake, now to your right, and another on your left, crossing the fenceline ahead by a gate close to the edge of the lake on your left. Pass through the gap in the tall row of conifers straight ahead to find yourself on the edge of a large field. The path across the field should start a little to the left of where you are standing. Cross the field diagonally to the far corner, initially

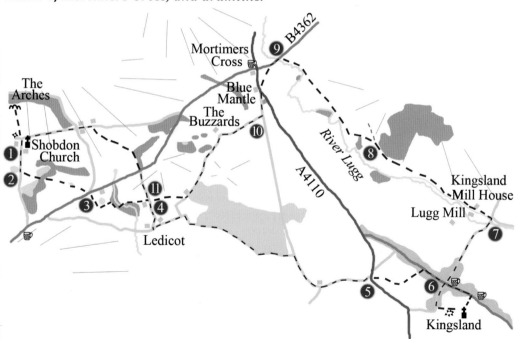

35

SHOBDON CHURCH

At the time of Domesday Shobdon was held by the Mortimers of nearby Wigmore, and in the 12th century they granted it to their steward, Oliver de Merlimond, who built a castle and founded an abbey to replace a wooden church. (The site of this castle lies some 120 yards west of the church, the motte being visible amongst some trees to the north of a car park, its bailey now under a chicken processing factory.) The monks seem to have had problems finding a decent water supply, and the abbey was moved to near Aymestrey, and then, perhaps when de Merlimond fell out with the Mortimers during the Anarchy, the Mortimers moved it to Wigmore where it very much became 'their' abbey. In the meantime, de Merlimond, who had been on pilgrimage to Santiago de Compostela, had set about lavishing decoration on his church. Many of its features were similar to those of churches in western France through which Oliver is known to have travelled, though it may be that the ideas reached Shobdon via Kilpeck church which is now thought to have been constructed shortly before that at Shobdon, rather than the other way round. Oliver was certainly a man of learning, entrusted with the education of the Mortimer heir, and it is likely that he knew the details of numerous illustrations contained in illuminated manuscripts. It is also probable that he took a great interest in and directed the work at Shobdon. Though now badly weathered, the features of the sculpture at Shobdon have been preserved in a set of lithographs made in 1852 and plaster casts which were photographed before most of them were destroyed in a fire at Crystal Palace in 1936, though one can still be seen in the cast court at the Victoria and Albert Museum in London.

The story now moves to the 1700s. Horace Walpole, son of Prime Minister Robert Walpole and friend of Richard Bateman (see the story of Shobdon Court overleaf), acquired Strawberry Hill, a villa set above the Thames in Richmond in 1749, and set about enlarging and elaborating it in a style that became known as Strawberry Hill Gothic. Richard Bateman, who had a villa further up the Thames at Old Windsor, decided that this was the style for a new church at Shobdon, and pulled down the old church (except for the tower), in an act that was viewed even then as vandalism. The new church, at a casual glance, looks from the outside like any number of village churches – until you notice the ogee-headed windows. Inside, the new church takes gothic flights of fancy in joinery and plasterwork, giving the visitor the impression of being amongst the decorations on a wedding cake.

The chancel arch and north and south doorways of the Norman church were re-erected to form a folly at the end of a tree-lined walk known as 'The Arches', where they have since weathered badly, recent restoration work aiming to prevent even further decay. In these reconstructed arches, one of the tympana depicts the Harrowing of Hell, the other Christ supported by four angels. The other carvings include patterns of interlace, serpents, human figures, birds, possible lions, stags and goats, some of the carvings and compilations being similar to those at Kilpeck. The Romanesque font is preserved in the new church, carved with four lions, and recently the occasional carved stone from the original church has been found to have been reused in the parapet of the new church.

SHOBDON COURT

Sir James Bateman acquired the manor of Shobdon in 1705. He was descended from John Bateman, a Fleming who had been naturalised during the reign of Charles II and a financier who made a fortune through the East India and South Sea Companies. Armed with this fortune, Sir James built a large Queen Anne mansion with a range of stables and formal gardens, together with a landscaped park. Sir James's son William became MP for Leominster and subsequently was ennobled as Viscount Bateman in 1725. Sir John Bateman, the second viscount, inherited the estate in 1744 and preferred to live in London. He therefore left the estate's management in the care of his uncle, Richard Bateman, a friend of Horace Walpole (see Shobdon church). Sir John died childless in 1802, the viscountcy dying with him, and the estate was inherited by William Hanbury, a descendant of the first viscount's sister, who took the name Bateman. He was subsequently ennobled as Baron Bateman, having served as MP for Northampton. New gardens were laid out in the mid 19th century. The title and the estate passed down two more generations through the male line, but when the third baron died childless in 1931, the title became extinct. The house became expensive to run and was demolished in 1933, leaving a pair of gate piers and 18th-century stableblock.

aiming at the right-hand edge of what appears to be a small scrubby copse in a hollow in the field but, as you near it, proves to be a fringe of vegetation around a ice age pond (see p.46). Keep this pond on your immediate left, then continue on much the same line to the right of the next group of trees and so on to a field gate out onto the B road. (If there is a crop in the field, you may need to walk round the edges, though the path through the crop may have been preserved.)

3 Cross the B road and go through the footpath gate (slightly hidden in the hedge) that heads into a campsite. Follow the hedgeline on your right and towards the end of the campsite walk between a fence on your left and the hedgeline on your right, to go through a footpath gate into the field beyond. Turn left here so that you keep the campsite on your left and walk along to the strip of woodland ahead. In the corner of the field, turn right, with the strip of woodland now on your left. After 100 yards or so, just before the top of the rise, the path turns left to cross the woodland, passing over a stream to reach a gate through which you pass to enter another field. Keep ahead and follow the field boundary on your right, soon passing close by a house also on your right, to leave the field by a gateway and drop down onto a minor road.

4 Turn right on the road and follow it along, ignoring a lane off to your left that leads to a farm, but turning left onto another road shortly after this. Follow this road

along, keeping right at the next two road junctions, but bearing left at the third where there are some cottages immediately on your left-hand side, following road signs for Kingsland. Follow this road along till you meet an A road on the edge of Kingsland.

5 Cross this and take the path up a few steps on the other side of the road (slightly to your right as you look across the road junction); cross a stile into a strip of woodland. Cross this and go over another stile into an orchard. Cross the orchard and the stile on the far side, then turn slightly right and cut across a corner of the field to another stile. Within a few yards you'll come to another stile on your left which you cross. The path technically crosses the field towards a bungalow built of yellowish bricks on the far side, but you may need to walk around the field edge to reach that point. Then walk down the short track to the right of the bungalow and turn right on the road. Shortly before you reach the crossroads, on the left is a house called Maples, once the site of Kingsland's theatre.

> **KINGSLAND THEATRE**
> The house now called Maples was once a barn, the first floor of which was used for theatre performances by the Kingsland Amateur Dramatic Society which flourished in the 1880s. The performances were popular, with as many as 500 people seeking admission, and the money raised helping to support the parish poor, the village school, and even the acquisition of a new fire engine.

6 Turn right at the crossroads and walk past the village hall to the bend in the road, where you take the footpath off to the left. This quickly leads into a field with the motte of Kingsland Castle on your right. Walk along the edge of the field to the church. At the church, turn left and walk down towards the 17th-century Angel Inn, passing the millennium green on your right. Turn left on the road and walk back to the crossroads, where you turn right and walk along the road and over the bridge across the Lugg.

7 Once across you quickly come to a road off to the right, opposite which you take the track to the left. At the bend ahead, go through the gate of Kingsland Mill House and continue until you reach a garage. Pass to the left of this through an arched gateway, and then cross the stile at the far end of the garage into a field. Cross this to the next stile ahead, keeping an eye out for the millwheel on the other side of the river (more clearly visible in winter when the trees are bare). This was a farm waterwheel which has been recently relocated here, having originally been fed by water from the wooden sluice and iron aqueduct that stands to the left of the path where it crosses the second stile. Lugg Mill, which stands between the leat and the river, is an 18th-century building which once had a waterwheel at each end. It ceased work in 1958 and was converted to a house in 1993-4. Most of the leat which served it has since been ploughed out.

KINGSLAND CASTLE

The castle site has the remains of a substantial motte and several baileys, the footpath to the church passing through one bailey, another lying to the right once you have passed the motte. Further ditches suggest that another enclosure might have lain to the left of the bailey you cross. To the south of the motte and across a stream are the remains of fishponds. Traces of stone-work on the motte suggest that it once supported an octagonal shell keep with towers at the angles, and a barbican or gatehouse on the north-east. It was probably built by the de Braoses, and tradition suggests that King John stayed here in 1216 in his campaigns against that family. John Leland in 1540 recorded that part of the keep was still standing, but the castle must have been beyond use well before then, for no mention is made of it in the events surrounding the nearby Battle of Mortimers Cross in 1461.

The king in the name Kingsland is believed to have been Merewalh, a ruler of the Magonsaetan in the 650s, who is said to have had a palace, a large open hall built of timber, in the vicinity. When he was converted to Christianity by the Northumbrian monk Edfrith, he gave extensive grants of land to found a nunnery in Leominster, but reserved the area around present Kingsland for himself.

KINGSLAND CHURCH

Largely built in the 1300s, the church is notable for the unusual Volka chapel (see photo on the left) at the entrance. It might have been used by penitents until such time as the parish priest would allow them back into the main church for communion. Its name may be a corruption of Walter, and a theory suggests that it was the burial place of Walter de Mortimer, parish priest in 1315, for the chapel contains an open tomb chest. The chancel has a fine collection of stained glass, that in the east window dating from the 14th century, and a roof ceiled and painted during a restoration by G.F. Bodley in the 1860s.

THE RIVER LUGG

The Lugg has been declared a Site of Special Scientific Interest, the area cited running from bank top to bank top, so including the open water together with fringing vegetation and exposed sediments. A mile long section was flattened by bulldozer at the end of 2020 in what appears to have been a mix-up of communication between the landowner, the parish council (concerned at flooding), Natural England, the Environment Agency and the Forestry Commission. The ramifications continue.

The section of river from Mortimers Cross to Leominster is classed as a transitional river type, being mainly a river passing through clay but also some coarse substrates. Upstream of Leominster there are pools and riffles over a gravel/cobble bed whereas downstream the river is deeper and travels slower over a clay/silt bed.

A survey of streams feeding the Lugg carried out by the Herefordshire and Radnorshire Nature Trust in 1983 revealed that many were of wildlife interest, particularly for higher plants and mosses. Aquatic plants included water-crowfoots, pondweeds and yellow water lily, with bankside vegetation composed of species such as water aven, great pond sedge, yellow flag and marsh speedwell. Unfortunately, since 1983 many of these streams have been affected at one time or another by dredging and use of herbicides. Changes in practice recently, and the new system of stewardship grants for farmers, should be reversing this trend – except for when a bulldozer is deliberately employed of course.

Once over this next stile, follow the path initially round the edge of the field to your left, the path shortly leading through a strip of woodland below a bank before re-emerging in the field. Keep following the edge of this very large field and eventually you'll come to a gate into the next field. Once in this field, the path slants up to the wood on your half-right to a point about 100 yards to the left of the corner of the wood nearest to you (see photo alongside). Once you reach the wood, keep this on your right and follow its edge to reach a gateway, just down from the corner of the field, into the next field.

8 There are two footpaths at this point, the route you want being the left-hand one, which leads straight across the almost flat part of the field to a point of woodland that rises up from the river. Here, the line of the path turns slightly left to pass just to the right of two oaks that stand in the field and crosses the field to a stile near the river. Over this stile, the path follows the fenceline on your left, with a grassy bank on your right. When you reach a gate into the next field, go through it and head straight across the field, aiming for the single large willow on its far side. Here, pass through a footpath gate to the willow's immediate right and cross a small bridge over a stream, and once over continue on the same line to the far side of the next field. Here you have a choice: you can take a permissive path that follows the meanders of the river on your left or follow the fenceline on your left that tops a bank, the two routes rejoining near the next gateway.

In the next field you quickly reach a stile on your left, which you cross, then following the river towards the road bridge ahead. Leave the field by a stile just to the right of the bridge.

9 Turn left on the road and cross the bridge, and almost immediately, just past the Mortimers Cross road sign, you will reach a footpath into the field on the left. Take the path diagonally across the field, aiming for a point slightly to the left of a cream-painted cottage called Blue Mantle (you'll see the sign on its gate when you reach it).

Leave the field by the stile on the far side, cross the A road and head down the minor road, with the Covenhope Valley off to your right (see Battle of Mortimers Cross information on next page).

10 Take the first lane off to the right near a Victorian house, and possibly signposted to 'The Buzzards', the name of a house. Walk up the slight rise and then down and past The Buzzards, following what is now more or a track up and over another slight rise. In a while you'll come to a black and white house on your right.

11 Immediately past this house, cross the stile and a plank bridge into the field on the right. The path crosses this field along the dip in the ground and through a footpath gate, to cross another field to a point just to the left of the red brick house on the far side. Leave the field by

THE BATTLE OF MORTIMERS CROSS

The Wars of the Roses began in the 1450s as a result of concerns about the state of the government under the ineffective Henry VI and his unpopular wife Margaret of Anjou, coupled with anger at the loss of all English possessions in France save Calais. Henry was childless, and in 1447 the death of his uncle and heir, Humphrey duke of Gloucester, made Richard duke of York (son of Richard earl of Cambridge and Anne Mortimer, the heir of the Mortimer family), heir presumptive. It was around him, therefore, that opposition to the king gathered. In 1452 he assembled an armed force with the intention of forcing aside Henry VI's most trusted adviser, Edmund Beaufort, duke of Somerset, whom York appears to have detested. Indeed it is this personal hatred that seems to have been the initial cause of the Wars of the Roses. However York showed himself to be almost as inept as Henry VI, and his attempt ended ignominiously in surrender at Dartford. Then, in October 1453, Margaret of Anjou produced a male heir in Prince Edward. Mistrust now fed mistrust and led, in 1455, to the first Battle of St Albans where York, supported by Warwick the Kingmaker, was victorious, and Somerset was killed. York briefly became Lord Protector, but he was soon out-manoeuvred by Queen Margaret and his government dismissed. In 1459 fighting broke out again as Margaret tried to separate York and Warwick from other potential support, whilst massively superior Royalist (Lancastrian) forces closed in on the Yorkists. The York army was joined by the earl of Salisbury (Warwick's father) after he had fought his way through a detachment of the Royal army at Blore Heath. At Ludford Bridge on the outskirts of Ludlow the two armies came face to face. The Yorkists, however, were dispirited and many of their men deserted, leading to the army dissolving overnight and its leaders fleeing. York went to Dublin, and Warwick and York's son, Edward earl of March, to Calais.

In 1460 Warwick recommenced operations and landed at Sandwich, entering London peaceably on 2 July, though the Tower initially remained in Lancastrian hands. The main Yorkist force then caught up with Henry VI at Northampton and took him prisoner, so establishing a Yorkist government under an obedient king. In September, York left Dublin and joined Warwick in London. Margaret of Anjou had meanwhile fled into Wales and in due course to Pembroke where she started to hatch plans with Jasper Tudor and raise an army. She then sailed to Scotland and from there went to the north of England to raise a second, larger, army. At Hull she gathered reinforcements to her already numerous northern Lancastrian levies by sea from Somerset and Devon. York decided to advance against this army, sending Edward earl of March to look after the Welsh Marches and leaving Warwick in London with the king. On 30 December York met defeat and death at the Battle of Wakefield.

As heir to the Yorkist claim to the throne, Edward, who had lost not just his father but also his brother in the battle, realised that first he must deal with the threat of Jasper Tudor, and to do this gathered his forces at Ludlow and Wigmore and chose a site that suited him on which to fight the battle. Historians still argue to this day about its precise whereabouts.

Ordnance Survey maps mark it just north-west of Kingsland, but a more likely site is near the modern crossroads at the Mortimers Cross Inn. Certainly, items of armour and weaponry have been found in the field to the south-west of the inn (which this walk crosses). Also here is a cottage called Blue Mantle, which was the name of Edward's herald, and the site of a large oak known as the Battle Oak. In practical terms, this site gave the Yorkists a defended flank on their left in the river Lugg, and a protective escarpment on their right which was probably then wooded. Bearing in mind Edward's tactics in later battles, he is likely to have placed archers in these woods to harry the Lancastrian lines, and may have hidden some cavalry up the Covenhope valley, or a smaller valley to the south on the line of the walk to The Buzzards, to release at a critical moment, as he did in the Battle of Tewkesbury in 1471. It also gave a front and battle plan that would be achievable with Edward's likely force of some 2,000 men.

The battle took place on 2 February, Candlemas, and the Yorkists were victorious. They were always the favourites to win: they were fighting on home ground, and they had a charismatic leader who was to prove himself an able strategist, and who told his men to regard the appearance of a parhelion (where two 'additional' suns appear in a halo of light around the sun in a particular set of extremely cold weather conditions) as a good omen for them. (Edward subsequently took the sign as a personal badge.) Yorkist losses were probably slight, Lancastrian ones heavy.

On 17 February Warwick met Margaret's northern army at the second Battle of St Albans, where he was defeated. His army badly mauled, and having lost the king to Margaret's army, Warwick retreated westwards. On hearing the news, Edward's army, now swollen in numbers, marched eastwards and the two forces met at Burford. Margaret's army had its own problems however. It was suffering desertion and had no siege train to tackle London, which remained loyal to the Yorkists, and Margaret retreated northwards. Warwick and Edward therefore marched to London where they were met by a relieved population and where, on 4 March, Edward was proclaimed king as Edward IV. But before there could be any coronation, York and Edward marched north in pursuit of Margaret's army. A fierce engagement at Ferrybridge on 28 March was followed by one of the largest battles ever fought on British soil, when 50,000 men engaged at Towton, in which the Lancastrians were slaughtered amongst flurries of snow. Edward was crowned king on 28 June.

DRUMLIN COUNTRY

Drumlins are formed of usually small stones and gravel that have been carried and then deposited by glaciers as they lose the capacity to keep carrying all the material they have gathered, due most likely to the warming of the atmosphere and melting of at least part of the glacier. However, the glacier must have still existed to give the drumlins their distinctive half-egg shape as it moved relentlessly forward, otherwise the material would have been haphazardly deposited blanket fashion. Drumlins indicate the direction of travel of the glacier; the steeper end of each drumlin is the one closer to the source of the glacier, the debris being smoothed out in the direction of flow. Such topography often includes pools or lakes, isolated from rivers and streams by the drumlins, such as those found from here westwards to Titley. The glacier that formed these drumlins would have been part of the ice sheet that covered much of western Herefordshire at the end of the last Ice Age. By around 17,000 BC this was beginning to retreat as the temperature warmed.

the stile and turn right on the lane, following this till you reach the B road ahead.

Cross this and go through the footpath gate into the corner of a field. Follow the field boundary on your right, the path passing through one field gateway near the bottom of the dip in the ground and then shadowing the route of what is probably an old sunken lane. If you look to your left on this section of the walk you will see an area of classic drumlin country. When this field boundary bends slightly to the right as you near a group of houses, cross the finger of the field to the left of the remnant of a large oak and leave the field to join a minor road. Turn left on the road and follow it to the crossroads ahead, continuing straight over and along the avenue of beeches to return to where you parked.

Walk 7
Weobley

5.25 miles, on tracks, field paths, B road and minor roads. A few stiles. Includes one of Herefordshire's Black and White villages, the sites of Weobley and Garnstone castles, the Ley (one of Herefordshire's finest timber-framed houses), and Weobley church.

1 With your back to the entrance of the Salutation Inn, turn right and walk up the road, turning right after a few yards onto a track that leads past a telephone kiosk. Go through the gate ahead into what was the outer bailey of Weobley Castle. Keep to the line indicated by the initial stretch of track and walk across the outer bailey and then the inner bailey,

A4112

Weobley

The Ley

B4230

Permissive path

Garnstone Park

Fenhampton

across the line of the moat on the far side and so to a kissing gate.

Go through the gate, then keep ahead to another gate at the far end of the meadow, walking roughly parallel to the hedge on your right. Go through the kissing gate on the far side and then follow the path that aims straight at the hillside. En route cross a track and go through another kissing gate.

WEOBLEY

Weobley, a borough, was granted several charters for markets and fairs, and these would have been held in the triangular market place in the middle of the village. A market hall stood here till it was pulled down on the orders of the Thynne family (see under WEOBLEY CASTLE overleaf) in the mid 1800s. The other buildings on this site, all timber-framed and including a nail producing workshop, burned down in 1943.

From 1295 to 1306 Weobley sent two Members to Parliament but after the voters complained about the expense of supporting them, no further MPs were sent until 1628. From then Weobley sent two MPs to Parliament until it lost them as a result of the Reform Act of 1832 (see also pp.52-4).

WEOBLEY CASTLE

Probably built by one of the de Lacy family, the castle featured in the Anarchy, the wars between Stephen and Matilda. In 1138 Geoffrey Talbot seized it in support of Gilbert de Lacy's claim to the de Lacy inheritance which had been denied by Stephen's predecessor, Henry I, and then took Hereford. Stephen reacted swiftly and soon retook Hereford, but meanwhile the earl of Gloucester, an illegitimate son of Henry I, had declared his support for Matilda, complicating military matters on the Marches. Talbot led a reprisal attack from Weobley on Hereford to punish the inhabitants for the support they had given Stephen, burning much of the city south of the Wye. Undeterred, Stephen laid siege to Weobley Castle and quickly captured it. Thereafter the castle passed through the hands of the de Braoses, Gamages, Verdons and Crophulls to the Devereuxs. In 1572 Walter Devereux was created earl of Essex, but when the title became extinct, the castle was bequeathed to Thomas Thynne, Viscount Weymouth, allowing one of the Thynne family to be one of Weobley borough's two MPs until the system of rotten boroughs was reformed.

A plan of the castle dated to 1655 shows a rectangular keep with round corner towers sitting inside a four-sided, not quite rectangular, bailey, again with round corner towers, together with D-shaped towers in the middle of the two longer sides. Two 'dwelling houses' stood in this bailey to the north of the keep. The entrance to the bailey seemed to have had no formal gatehouse, although the cellar of the Corner House, at the entrance from the village to the castle site, has a massive stone fireplace in the cellar and might have once been part of a guardroom for the castle entrance. All the stonework of the castle above ground level has been taken for use elsewhere (look at some of the stone-built houses in Weobley!), though stone remains buried in some of the earthworks. Archaeological survey work in recent years has shown that the bailey fell out of use in the 13th century. By the 14th century, part had been laid out as burgage plots, but by the 16th the site had been handed over to agricultural use with ridge and furrow field systems developing. To further complicate analysis of the earthworks, huts and an air raid shelter were built on part of the site during the Second World War. It is clear that the keep was at the far end of the site, the most extensive remains of the surrounding ditch being at this end and on the east. The limits of the bailey are less easy to pick out on the west.

GARNSTONE CASTLE

Garnstone was the home of the Tomkyns family from the mid 16th century, and they probably built their house on the site of an earlier one. In 1661, the estate was sold to Colonel Birch (for whom see WEOBLEY CHURCH, p.52), who carried out various alterations. That building was demolished when Samuel Peploe built a house to the design of John Nash further down the hillside. This house, Garnstone Castle, was demolished in 1958. A large circular flat-topped mound surrounded by a ditch lies close to this later building, and might either be the motte of an earlier castle or the result of landscaping the park. A walled garden, with hothouses, peach house, fig house and vineries, lay to the west of the house; elements of this survive, as do many of the trees planted for the parkland and deer park.

2 When you reach the trees which shelter the remains of Garnstone Castle, turn right and follow the fence line. When the path is crossed by a gate, follow the fence line for about 50 yards, then cross a stile onto a track. Go past a red brick house and when you reach the end of a tall brick wall, go through a kissing gate on the left and walk across the field diagonally to the far corner.

3 In that corner, go through a gate and after about 50 yards turn right through a second one. Go straight ahead up the hill and keep following the wide gravelled track you're on when it turns right. When this track splits, take the right-hand fork and follow it through a gate into the wood. Carry on through the wood, where the gravelled track becomes a grassy ride. This ride passes through woodland, then runs just above a field on your right before re-entering woodland.

4 About 40 yards into the woodland, before the track starts to bend to the right, take the footpath that heads left, somewhat back on yourself, up the hill and then zig-zags through a narrow gulley. At the top, turn right along the permissive path bordered by beech trees. In due course you will pass a trig point on your right, and soon after

that, you will reach a junction of paths. Ignore the track that leads down to the right and keep going straight on, to head steeply down the narrow woodland path. At the bottom of the slope, your path crosses a track; when you reach another track (almost straightaway), turn left onto it. It emerges from the wood and turns left, then after a few yards you turn right down a footpath which then joins a tarmacked track which you follow down to the B road.

5 Turn right on the road and about 300 yards past a cottage on the right, take the gravelled track to the left which leads towards Fenhampton Farm. Just past the farm, the track comes to an end at a gateway into a field ahead. Go through the gateway and turn right along the permissive path which runs along the field edge; keep following it round the corner of the field until you get to a footpath sign to the right, where you turn right.

[If the permissive path is no longer permitted, return along the track for a few yards and turn right to follow a path along a hedgerow that will be on your right. At the far end of the field, walk along the edge of the wood on your left. About 100 yards before the cottage you can see in front of you, turn right along a path between fields. Keep following the path until you reach the end of the field on your right. At the corner of the field, cross the next field, bearing slightly right and heading just to the right of the farm buildings you can see. As you approach the wood you'll notice a footbridge and gate.]

THE LEY
The house was built in 1589 to an H-plan with east and west wings by Charles Brydges, a member of a family that had owned the site since at least 1428. In the 16th century the size of the estate was much increased, only to be gradually sold off to the point that by 1702 little remained. The house then became part of the Garnstone estate for a while.

6 Cross the footbridge and go through the gate, then carry on up the path straight ahead, keeping to a hedge on your right. It gains a concrete surface and then enters the farmyard. Keep to the left of the farm buildings – there may be some metal gates to pass through – and follow the lane round to the front of The Ley.

7 Opposite the house, and just past a pond on the left, cross a stile into a small triangular field and follow the hedge on the left. Go through two gates at the end of the field (one each side of the end of a track) into a long field and this time walk along the hedge on your right. At the end of this field, go through a kissing gate into another field. Walk along the hedge on your right and when it turns right keep ahead to the far side of the field. Don't cross the stile here, but turn right and follow the hedge on your left down to a kissing gate further along the hedgerow. Go through this and cross the field, heading slightly right, to another kissing gate. Once through this, walk across the field to the corner of the fence on the far side, and go through the gate here. Follow the path ahead, which will lead you into a farmyard through which you follow the track which will bring you round in a curve to a gate beside a partially timber-framed, partially breeze-block building. Walk through the gates adjacent to this into Weobley.

Turn right onto the lane, then immediately left to return to the Salutation Inn. From here you can walk down the main street to the road junction at the bottom, and keep going straight on to reach the churchyard and visit the church (see overleaf).

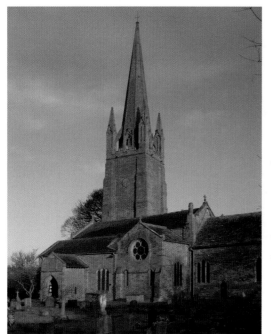

WEOBLEY CHURCH

Weobley church spire protrudes above the gentle nearby hills, and can be seen from miles away, looking somewhat like a child's drawing of a space rocket with flying buttresses connected to the pinnacles at the tower corners. The church has two aisles and is a mix of styles, with a Norman south doorway, an Early English chancel with Perpendicular east window, whilst much of the nave is in the Decorated style. In the chancel are a number of memorials that provide links to major episodes of local history.

JOHN BIRCH

Near the altar stands a memorial to Colonel John Birch. Born in Ardwick, near Manchester, to a family of minor gentry status, he had little formal education but acquired his father's Presbyterian beliefs. At 18 he moved to Bristol, entered the wine trade, married the widow of a wealthy grocer and established himself as a merchant (some claim that he had started work as a humble packman). He lost his business when Prince Rupert captured Bristol in 1643, and joined the Parliamentary cause. A fearless soldier, he fought with distinction at the second Battle of Newbury

and at the last battle of the first Civil War at Stow-on-the-Wold. Having managed to become Governor of Bath, he sought advancement by hatching a plot to seize Hereford by hiding men in a wagon in the depth of winter, the men emerging when one of the city gates was reached, overpowering the guard and allowing the remainder of Birch's force to enter and seize the city. He thereupon became its governor. Being a merchant, managing finances for personal gain came naturally to him. He now acquired Hereford Castle, but with disbandment of much of the army realized no profit could be made from renting it out for garrisoning troops, so sold it to the county for £600. Constantly nagging

Parliament for payment of monies he felt were due to him, he seems to have been paid for all his losses, costs and more, at the same time obtaining what can only be called bribes from individuals so as not to put their estates forward for sequestration as supporters of the king. Using his gains to acquire land and property in Herefordshire, he turned from soldier to wealthy land-owner and politician, being elected as MP for Leominster in 1646, and then, having acquired the Garnstone estate, for Weobley four times between 1679 and 1690. He was amongst those who rode to greet William Prince of Orange when he landed in Weymouth prior to being asked to take the throne as king.

SIR WALTER DEVEREUX

Sir Walter Devereux died on 25 June 1402 from wounds received at the Battle of Pilleth three days earlier. This battle was fought between English forces under Sir Edmund Mortimer, and Welsh forces either commanded by Owain Glyndwr in person, or his lieutenant Rhys Gethin. The English were roundly defeated, partly because it appears that their Welsh archers switched sides during the battle, with far reaching consequences for the next few years. Firstly, Sir Edmund was to join with Glyndwr

and marry one of his daughters, which confused loyalties along the central Marches and, secondly, the English side of the border was laid open to Welsh raids and even general banditry. It took up to five years to restore law and order and full English control during which time many properties were burnt to the ground and several churches despoiled. Walter Devereux had served as an esquire to Richard II in a fruitless expedition against Scotland in 1385, was knighted by 1391 and went to Ireland with Richard II in September 1394. He served as Sheriff of Herefordshire in 1401, a year in which he was also a Member of Parliament. His wife Agnes Crophull was, by her second husband John Parr, the great-great-grandmother of Katherine Parr, the last wife of King Henry VIII.

ALICE CROPHULL & SIR JOHN MERBURY

John Merbury, who died in 1438, was the third husband of Alice Crophull. Merbury was a trusted servant of the Lancastrian dynasty, starting with John of Gaunt, then his son Henry IV, his son Henry V and finally his son Henry VI. He was given many official appointments, including being made Sheriff of Herefordshire on several occasions. He was first elected to Parliament in 1419, and again in 1421, 1425 and 1427.

WEOBLEY HOUSES

Behind the Red Lion (which has recently become an Indian restaurant called 'Lal Bagh' – Red Lion in Bengali) is a cruck-framed cottage whose main frame comprises pairs of large curved timbers, each pair usually being halves of the same tree. Cruck-framed houses are some of the oldest timber-framed houses and usually date from the 1300s.

The Old Grammar School on Hereford Road was founded in 1659 by William Crowther, and would have been a school for the sons of the local middle classes. (The close-set timber framing is an indication of the wealth of those who built it.) The school rooms were on the ground floor, whilst the upstairs rooms comprised a dormitory for the boys and rooms for the master. By 1717 the grammar school accommodated up to 25 boys.

The Throne, on the corner of Gadbridge Road and Hereford Road, is a two-storey timber-framed house built in the late 16th or early 17th century. Some of the stonework in the house is of medieval date and probably came from the nearby castle site. An inscription that was found in the fireplace says that the house was built in 1599. King Charles I is supposed to have stayed here on 5 September 1645 – hence the name of the house.

The Unicorn Inn in the High Street is of two storeys with attics, and was built in the 17th century.

Walk 8
Lingen & Limebrook

5.5 miles, largely on a mixture of woodland tracks and paths, paths across meadows and minor roads. Only the occasional stile. Includes the site of Limebrook Priory, Kinsham Court, and an optional visit to Lingen Castle motte and deserted medieval village.

Park near the Royal George Inn in Lingen (GR 365 670).

1 Walk down the road with the church behind you and the pub on your left, and pick up the footpath that passes between Rose & Ivy Cottages and Brook House on the left and enters a small field by a gate. This field is pock-marked with bumps and hollows, those nearest the road most likely remnants of the medieval and post-medieval village, whilst those nearer the stream may indicate some system of water management. Follow the fenceline on your right and the path soon bends to the right and then crosses a series of streams by four bridges to join a wide track at the foot of the woodland that rises above the streams (ignore a path that leads off to the right as you cross the series of bridges). Turn right on the track. Keep right at the first fork and follow the track alongside a row of conifers and then uphill.

2 Again bear right at the next fork as you reach the grounds of the white-painted Lingen Hall (built in the mid 1800s). The path then follows the edge of the gardens of the hall.

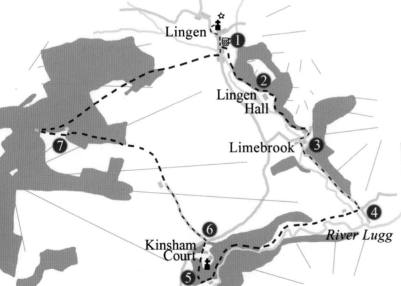

Lingen

Lingen Hall

Limebrook

River Lugg

Kinsham Court

55

LIMEBROOK PRIORY

This nunnery of Augustinian canonesses was founded during the reign of Richard I, probably by one of the Mortimers or Lingens; the Mortimers had already founded an Augustinian Monastery at Wigmore. Augustinians took their name from St Augustine of Hippo (392-430) and were less ascetic than many of their counterparts, and given to 'good works' such as running hospitals for lepers and retreats for the elderly and acting as schoolteachers. The current remains consist of upstanding parts of the rubble walls of a building running east/west and probably dating from the 13th century. It is not known what part of the priory this formed, nor is it possible to work out an arrangement of buildings from the mounds that lie in the field to the east and north. The nearby cottage almost certainly includes re-used building material from the priory; indeed the curved south wall may represent part of one of the priory's buildings. It was probably always a small community, and had just six nuns at the time of its dissolution in 1539. Asarabacca, a species of wild ginger (unrelated to the spice), grows extensively on the slopes near Limebrook Priory and might have been cultivated by the nuns, for this groundcover plant with large, dark-green, kidney-shaped evergreen leaves and dull purple flowers in the spring, used to be used as an emetic and was believed to cure diseases of the ear. It was also used as a spice or a flavouring.

Beyond the hall the track drops down and then rises to reach a crossroads of tracks. Turn right and this track will bring you back to the edge of the woodland. Follow the track alongside the stream, next to which at one point you will see signs of the old millstream. The track becomes a narrow path which eventually rises up a bank and leaves the woodland by a small gate. Turn right on the track down to the farm buildings. Go through a gate and turn right on the track past the farm and follow it to a junction with a minor road.

3 Turn left on this, and beyond the house on the corner, keep a lookout for the remains of Limebrook Priory on the left: a section of stone walling right alongside the road, together with other walling remains in the field, and assorted humps and bumps in the ground. Continue along the road for about a third of a mile until it starts to make a 90-degree bend to the left and meets a road junction signed Upper Lye and Aymestrey.

4 Don't walk quite as far as the junction. Just before it, turn right onto a farm track and cross the bridge over the stream. Carry on along the track, keeping the buildings on your right. Go straight on past the farm to a gate across the track. Immediately through the gate, head up the bank on your left to a small gate into the field that lies above the river Lugg. Head down the bank and turn right to walk alongside its lower edge, to pass close to the river at one point and then head for a gate at the right-hand end of the hedge on the far side of the field. Go through the field gate and diagonally cross the field to a footpath gate at the left-hand end of the fenceline. Go through the two gates here, crossing a ditch between them. Then cross the next field to a gate just above the river that leads onto a path through the woodland beyond. Follow this track/path between the river and the foot of the slopes on your right, on which is perched Kinsham Court. The path eventually passes a cottage on the left and becomes a tarmacked lane.

⑤ About 100 yards past the cottage (and before you reach the road at the far end of the track), turn right on the footpath up through the woods. This will soon lead you to a fenceline. Kinsham Court and its chapel lie on

LINGEN

The name derives from a pre-English word for a stream, possibly one that means 'stream with clear water'. After the Norman Conquest the settlement was held by one Turstin from the Mortimers, from whom it passed to the Lingen family. The church dates from the late Victorian period, although the tower is older, possibly dating from the 16th century. The castle, reached by taking the public footpath that leaves the north side of the churchyard, consists of a prominent circular motte with a rectangular bailey to the west. There are indications on the surface of the motte that it may have once supported a shell keep with a gatehouse on the western side, whilst the bailey appears to have been defended by a ditch and a curtain wall, partially exposed in a modern cutting. To the north side of the castle are earthworks that represent the remains of a medieval village.

KINSHAM COURT & CHAPEL

Formerly part of the estate of the Harleys, the earls of Oxford, Kinsham Court was originally a hunting lodge and dower house. Florence Nightingale spent part of her childhood here and Lord Byron lived here in 1812-13, and wrote the first two cantos of *Childe Harold*. Jane Harley, wife of the 5th earl of Oxford, lived nearby at Titley. She was a friend of the Princess of Wales and frequently acquired lovers from among the pro-Reform party during her marriage, first Francis Burdett and then Byron in the aftermath of his affair with Caroline Lamb. He was 14 years her junior, and when she and her husband went abroad in 1813, Byron did not follow as she had hoped, but he did leave Herefordshire. In the 20th century Kinsham Court was owned by Sir John Arkwright (of the textile family). The chapel dates from around 1300, though the windows have since been renewed.

the far side of the field, but you follow the path that turns along the fenceline before the gate, then head to the left of the stone wall and the house. Cross the driveway and head towards the Wellingtonia with its soft bark (also known as a punch tree) behind which you'll find a stile on the footpath. Cross this and follow the (sometimes overgrown) field path straight ahead which passes outbuildings to the right. In about 20 yards it joins a track on which you continue ahead, then crosses a footbridge to emerge on to a minor road through a kissing gate.

6 Turn right on the road and after a few yards, left onto a lane. On the left a view of will open up of the hill on which stands Wapley hillfort (see photo alongside). After about a quarter of a mile, where the tarmacked lane becomes a stony track by a farm, keep to the right to follow the track around the hillside. When you reach a fork, keep left and further on ignore the track to the left and keep ahead. This track will eventually pass through a gate to lead into a field. Keep following the hedge on your left to reach another gate above a corner of woodland. Go through this gate and after some 30 yards, go through the gate on the right into the woodland and turn left on the path that follows the edge of the trees and then bears right. After about 100 yards there's a fork – take the left-hand path. Keep following the path straight ahead through the woodland, near the far end of which you need to bear slightly left uphill to leave it through a gate.

WAPLEY HILLFORT
This is a multivallate Iron Age hillfort, with up to three ditches and associated banks; it originally had two entrances. It is one of the many hillforts credited with being the site of Caratacus' final stand against the Romans. The pillow mounds within the hillfort are probably the result of the area being farmed for rabbits in the medieval period.

7 The footpath continues across the field towards a corner of woodland that juts into the field and then heads towards a house in another corner of the woodland. Go through the gate by the house and turn almost back on yourself on the track which initially shadows the fence between the woodland and the field that you've just crossed.

This track soon bends slightly left and heads more into the woodland, to eventually pass out by a kissing gate into a field. Cross this field on the embanked line of an old field boundary which roughly follows the contours of the ground straight across the field. As you cross the field you will pass an old hedgerow which you keep to your right. When you reach the end of the field you pass through the line of the old hedgerow to turn left on a track that leads back into the woodland through a gate.

Keep on the line of this track, which will narrow to the width of a sunken path, and it will lead you back into Lingen. When you reach the road, turn left to return to the Royal George Inn.

If you want to visit the church, carry on down the road. There is a path from the other side of the churchyard that leads to the castle site.

2 Leominster
& the castles and hillforts of north-east Herefordshire

LEOMINSTER

Once the priory had been established (see pp.64-5) a market soon sprang up near the entrance to the priory precincts, focussed on what is now Corn Square, the main gateway lying to the north of the square near the Forbury Chapel, which started its life as the chapel by the gateway. A borough was founded under Henry I (as also at Ledbury, Bromyard and Ross) with the creation of burgesses, freemen who paid an annual rent for their plot and elected some of their number to manage the affairs of the borough. These burgage plots were laid out around the usual wedge-shaped marketplace which in Leominster's case lay between Drapers Lane, the High Street and the southern end of Broad Street (see also LEDBURY, p.134). This area was soon encroached upon by various trades that grouped themselves around the narrow lanes still called Ironmongers Lane and Cordwainers Lane (the latter for shoemakers and leather workers), as well as the Butchery, now called Victoria Street. Etnam Street was created as the new east/west route; the previous one had run along the edge of the priory's precinct. School Lane was created as a piece of speculative building in the 15th century after a number of burgage plots alongside Corn Square had come under one ownership. The buildings on the corner of the square and School Lane nearest WH Smith were redeveloped to provide shop frontage along the new School Lane, with overhanging first-floor projections on both frontages. Indeed, much of Leominster was renewed in the period from 1450 to 1500, and as you walk through the streets it is worth looking up above the ground-floor shop fronts to see examples of carved bargeboards, decorative finials etc. Leominster town centre has over 200 listed buildings.

Leominster's prosperity was long based on the wool trade; the wool of the county's native breed, the Ryeland, was sometimes referred to as 'Lemster ore'. Michael Drayton wrote:

> Where lives the man so dull on Britain's furthest shore
> To whom did never sound the name of Lemster ore
> That with the silkworm's web for smallness doth compare?

The success of Leominster's market encouraged Hereford and Worcester to reschedule their market days to compete with Leominster and redirect the flow of trade. Nevertheless, Leominster flourished into the 18th century. But with the increasing industrial-scale production of cloth and textiles, the wool trade suffered and the town declined. Attempts to link Leominster to the canal system were unsuccessful, but for a brief period barges managed to use the river Lugg (and its connection with the Wye) to ferry goods to and from the town. The railway reached Leominster in 1853 and trains on the Marches line between Manchester and Cardiff still stop at Leominster station.

Walk 9
Leominster

3.25 miles, largely on field edge paths, tracks and roads. A few stiles (essentially on Eaton Hill). Includes Leominster town centre, the priory and Eaton Hill. You may want to check the opening times for Leominster Museum and the Grange (see below).

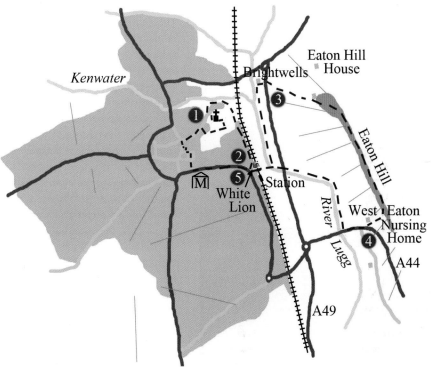

❶ The walk starts at Leominster Priory church. With your back to the entrance doorway to the priory church, turn right and right again to walk along the outside of the west face to the doorway under the tower and observe the carvings of the Herefordshire School on the capitals. Then, turn your back to this door and walk along the wall on your right and leave the churchyard by a gate in the corner of the wall. Then, walk back alongside the wall on a lane towards the west end of the church, turning left when adjacent to it down the lane to the Pinsley Mead picnic area by the river Kenwater.

Walk alongside the stone-built Priory House on your right (which may have been either the prior's house or the infirmary), built over the canalised Pinsley Brook which was used to flush away effluent from the lavatories sited above it. It was built *c.*1200-25 and modified in the early

PRIORY CHURCH

The church was founded c.660 after the conversion by Edfrith, a Northumbrian monk, of Merewalh, king of the Magonsaete, a mixed Saxon and British people then occupying much of Herefordshire. Their 'capital' was at Kingsland (see Walk 6). Merewalh granted Edfrith a large estate, some 12 miles across, on which to build his church, and he chose a typically Saxon 'island' spot, with rivers on two sides – the Kenwater and Pinsley to the north and the Lugg to the east – with the Arrow just a few miles to the south. The precinct of the church was marked by the rivers to the north and east, and by a large earthen bank to the south and west, this still remaining a prominent feature of the townscape along the edge of the cricket ground to the south of the church. By 690 Merewalh's sons had moved the centre of their kingdom from Kingsland to Hereford, where a cathedral was established, and the importance of Leominster declined. Little is known of the church's next 300 years, with only two mentions in surviving documents, but by c.1000 it appears to have become a nunnery (or possibly a monastery and nunnery for a while) run on Benedictine lines, having survived the Danish wars seemingly unscathed and having secured a wealth of important relics. Sometime after 1086 the nunnery fell into disrepute, and may even have been abandoned or closed down until it was refounded by Henry I in a charter of 1125 as a daughter house and priory to his abbey at Reading, where he was to be buried. The priory was to be an important royal staging post when travelling between the royal castle at Hereford (see pp.192-3) and the Lacy fief at Ludlow.

The building now comprises a Norman nave built in the 1120s and early 1130s as the parish church (the monks' church comprised the east end, transepts, crossing and easternmost part of the north aisle, which were all demolished after the Dissolution), a narrow north aisle some of which may belong to the Saxon predecessor, a south nave that is slightly wider than the Norman nave and was built in the Early English style to replace an existing aisle and consecrated in 1239, and a Decorated south aisle built in the 1320s which makes lavish use of ball-flower decoration on the outside. The tower was (re)built in the 15th century.

It is worth having a close look at the Norman nave. Strangely, it is not completely aligned with the presbytery and the high altar, perhaps because it was built adjacent to the Saxon church (and using its structure for the north aisle) which took a slightly different alignment. Then, a pair of arches of the nave are infilled with massive walling, leaving a much narrower arch. Why? If you look at the second pair of arches towards the east end, you can see that these are narrower and less high than those to either side. This has led to the suggestion that originally these arches would have had massive infilling stonework and a narrower arch, with the intention that the structure would have supported a domed stone roof like the one at Fontevrault Abbey in France, which has other similarities with Leominster Priory, or a barrel vault, or a groin vault. At high level in the nave look out for remnants of the red wall decoration which would once have covered the interior. Also of great interest is the 7ft-diameter Wheel of Life painted c.1275 on the north wall of the western bay of the nave, discovered during the church's restoration in the 1860s.

The church is home to work of the Herefordshire School (see p.221), on both the inside and outside of the west doorway and the capitals of the west window (less easily seen). Make sure you spot the small carving of Samson and the Lion on one of the north capitals on the inside of the doorway. This doorway has given rise to much speculation. It is slightly pointed on the outside (an early forerunner to Gothic architecture), but rounded on the inside. This is a feature of some churches in France, which is where the idea may have come from, but a case has also been made that the external doorway was re-used from elsewhere, perhaps when the tower was built, and that the odd alignment of some of the carved stones is a result of being reset. But it is not unusual to find carved stones in their original settings slightly mis-set. The building is full of interesting conundrums.

14th century. The building later became Leominster's Poor House, and most recently a youth hostel. Continue walking alongside the buildings, then keep ahead on the main path. This now takes a meandering course through a grassy area, passing a new 'stone circle' and a gateway made by Herefordshire artist Walenty Pytel (see p.244) into a play area. Turn left before the gateway and follow the path to join a road between the railway line and some new houses. When the road bends right, stay close to the railway line to then enter the yard of the White Lion inn. Walk across the yard, passing to the right of the inn.

❷ Immediately past the inn, take the footpath off to the left and over the footbridge across the railway line. Cross the river Lugg too, and then immediately turn left to walk through a field close to the river's bank and then between the river and an auction yard on your right. Follow the river till you reach the bridge that carries the access road to Brightwells auctions. Here, go through the kissing gate onto the access road, then the stile on your immediate right (before the main gates) to cross into Brightwells' yard. Walk across this, heading round just to the right of the main office block to reach a kissing gate through which you pass to emerge on the edge of Leominster's bypass.

❸ Cross the bypass and take the lane on the far side that heads towards a new house on the lower slopes of Eaton Hill ahead. You'll see a yellow brick building, also known as Eaton Hill, on your left (see photo alongside).

EATON HILL

Tradition has it that King Merewalh had a 'castle' at the northern end of the ridge, known as Comfort Castle, and there used to be some earthworks, long since gone. Leominster folk used to hold annual sports here, but that tradition died out, later replaced with the establishment of walks further along the hill, the remnants of which our walk follows. These were probably laid out by Thomas Burlton, who built the yellow-brick Eaton Hill in the 1860s or '70s and created what was probably the last, albeit small, deer park in Herefordshire. He also laid out gardens around the house; sale particulars in 1929 describe lawns, ornamental trees, shrubberies with walks, summerhouses and a walled garden. The house has subsequently been divided into flats.

Just past the new house, go through the footpath gate and then take a footpath on the left that leaves what has now become a track. Head up and across the hillside, passing through some woodland to reach a fence near the crest of the hill. Turn right in front of this fence, and follow it along to cross over the track near a transmitter station and then some stiles to emerge in a field. Keep on walking along the line of the hill, with the fenceline now on your right. As you approach the end of the field, the path leaves the field and slopes down and across the hillside to cross a stile. After a few more yards, take the path off to your right that heads steeply down the hillside through a young wood, the path passing some old stone steps and then becoming a wide grassy track that leads downhill to a stile that leads you out onto the A44.

④ Turn right on the A44 and cross the entrance and exit driveways of West Eaton nursing home, and then take the stile onto a path that shadows the A road. You soon reach the Lugg where you turn right and follow the bank of the river (ignoring any paths off to the right) to pass under the bypass where there is a butterfly mosaic to be seen.

The mosaic, designed by Janice Barrett, was created by reputedly 1,900 volunteers during the summer of 2006. Continue on this path back to the combination of river bridge and railway line bridge that you used before, and once again cross these.

5 When you reach the road junction, turn right on the main road and follow the bend of the road to walk up Etnam Street and into Leominster. Keep going till you approach a pedestrian crossing near Leominster Museum (on the other side of the road). (The museum tells the history of the town and is open from Monday to Saturday 10 to 4, but best to check: www.leominstermuseum.org.uk.)

To continue the walk, turn right down School Lane which will bring you into Corn Square. On the far side of the square, walk down Drapers Lane with its arched sign at its entrance. About halfway down the short lane, on the left, you will come to an alley called Cordwainers Lane. Go down this and emerge into High Street. Turn right here till you come to a crossroads.

Ahead of you is Broad Street with its cluster of cafés and antique shops, but to follow this walk, turn right into Church Street. Shortly you'll see the 13th-century Forbury Chapel on the left-hand side. Then the Priory

will come into view. Don't head straight for it, though; turn right down Pinsley Road and go straight on to reach the green lawns of the Grange. Look to the left across the grass and you'll see the recently restored Grange Court, now open for visitors. To return to the Priory, with your back to the front of Grange Court turn right and walk straight on back along the path.

GRANGE COURT

The timber-framed market hall built by John Abel in 1633 was originally known as the Butter Crosse and stood, with the ground floor as open space, at the top of Broad Street, for the sale of butter, eggs and chickens. It was dismantled in the mid 1800s, even then getting in the way of traffic, bought by John Arkwright and reassembled on The Grange, being modified and leased out as a family home with the name Grange Court. It was bought by Leominster District Council in 1939 to save it from being dismantled a second time and used as council offices until 2008 when it passed to a new community charity which took on its management and maintenance. It promotes itself as a community heritage and enterprise hub that also has a café. It is open between Tuesday and Friday from 10 to 12, but best to check: www.grangecourt.org.

Walk 10 Kimbolton

6.25 miles, largely on minor roads, paths across and along field edges and tracks. There are a few stiles and one long ford, though there is a footbridge and path along the bank above it. Includes a hillfort, a large dovecote and you might choose to visit Stocktonbury Gardens.

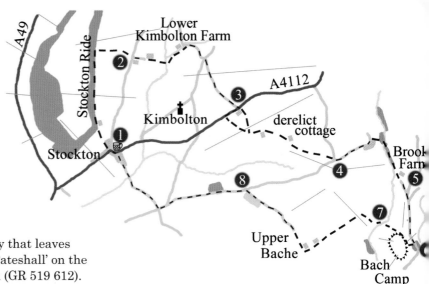

Park near the start of the footpath / bridleway that leaves the A4112 alongside the road signposted to 'Pateshall' on the bend near the Stockton Cross Inn in Stockton (GR 519 612).

STOCKTON RIDE

This is the line of a Roman road that ran northwards from Stretton Grandison via Bodenham, possibly converging with that which ran north from near *Magnis*, the main Roman centre near the more recent Hereford, to the north of Ashton. Recent archaeological work suggests that Stockton was a place of some importance in the 5th-7th centuries.

---

❶ Walk up the footpath/bridleway (initially a gravel track) along Stockton Ride, keeping straight ahead when it forks near a house. Adjacent to the next house the track becomes a footpath. Keep straight ahead, passing orchards of standard apple trees on your right. Once past the orchards, cross the first stile on the right that you come to, reached just beyond a boundary between two fields on the right and at a point where there is only a fence between the path and the field concerned. Once across the stile the path crosses the field to a stile some 30 yards to the left of the bottom right-hand corner of the field, the path staying some 30 yards out into the field from the hedgerow on your right. Over the stile – you may find it easier to use the field gate to the left of the stile – cross the next field, following the hedgerow on your right to another stile near a gate on the far side. Cross the stile and then follow a short track through a narrow field and so come to a road.

2 Cross the road and walk down the lane. Ignore the turnings to left and right and keep ahead along a short length of track to reach a field gate. Go through this and keep alongside farm buildings on your left, crossing a track that leads from the farmyard. Go through the gate into the field beyond the farm buildings and follow the field boundary on your right along to a bridge in the valley bottom. Cross the bridge and walk to the first telegraph pole some 20 yards beyond the bridge. Here, turn left to walk along the foot of a bank and field boundary to a gate in a corner of the field. Through this gate, walk along the path above the stream on your left, which emerges onto a track alongside Lower Kimbolton Farm. Follow the track and when it meets a road, turn right. Follow this and then take the first road turning to the left. This quickly leads to a crossroads which you go straight over. Follow this road up to the A4112.

3 At this point you have a choice, depending on whether a track (which is not a definitive path) is open. If it is, cross the road and go through the gateway to the immediate left of a cottage, to then follow this track alongside a hedgerow on your left to the end of the field. If the track is closed off, turn right on the main road and cross the stile on the left, reached shortly before the village sign for Kimbolton. Follow the hedgerow on your left for 100 yards before crossing it by a stile, and then head diagonally across this next field to its far corner. At this point the two routes meet. In the corner of the

field go through the double gate, then immediately take the gate on your left and turn right onto a track. This almost immediately makes a 90 degree turn to the left. Go through the gate at the end of the track and follow the hedge on your left to a small gate out onto a lane. Cross the lane and follow the hedge opposite, keeping it to your left and a cottage to your right. Cross a stile and a small paddock to another stile. Over this stile, the path divides. Take the path that heads almost diagonally across the field you are in, aiming to the right of a derelict cottage on the far side. The farmer here usually creates a path through the crop which should be obvious to follow. Cross the field boundary in front of the cottage and continue ahead across the next field to a stile, keeping to the left of a large solitary oak that stands in the field. Across this stile, the path crosses this next field diagonally, passing out of it by a gateway in the far corner onto a road.

4 Cross this road and take the one signposted 'Bache Deep Ford Unsuitable for Vehicles'. Follow this road as it curves round to the left in a few hundred yards past a group of houses that includes Bache Barn, The Bache and Lower Bache House and some converted barns. Immediately past these houses and a gravelled entrance to a parking area, you want to take the track on the right that heads downhill and is indicated by a sign that says 'Unsuitable for motor vehicles'. This track leads down to the previously warned of ford (there is a footbridge and path above it), and you keep on the track as it rises up the other side of the stream. In due course you emerge onto tarmac by the buildings of Brook Farm.

5 Follow the road, keeping the farm buildings on your left. Soon you'll catch glimpses of Bach Hillfort ahead and slightly to the right. Keep on the road, following it up to a little ridge (ignoring two turnings off to the left) and then gently down, passing below the hillfort on your right. Shortly after you reach some woodland on your left you'll meet the Herefordshire Way, which crosses the road.

6 Turn right onto this, passing through a kissing gate into a tussocky field – the tussocks created by ants. Cross this uphill to reach a gate which leads you out into the ditch of the hillfort. Turn right and follow the ditch (following the field boundary on your right), it presently bringing you onto the crest of the ridge, with the main ramparts of the hillfort to your left. From here your route is straight downhill aiming for the far right-hand corner of the field, where you cross a brook by a bridge.

in which, after about 100 yards, you reach a gateway on your right through which you pass and leave the gravelled track. Once through the gateway, follow the field boundary on your left to reach the top corner of the field and find a gateway onto a track. Take this track and after a while it will lead past a house on your left to join a tarmacked lane near a group of houses that includes Humber Court.

2 Turn left on this lane and just before you reach the church on the left, turn right on a lane which will lead you in an arc around the long line of barns that are part of Humber Court. Where the lane bends left, bear right and then almost immediately left round a corrugated iron-clad barn to walk up to a gateway into a field. Once in this field, walk ahead up the gentle slope to the far corner, in effect the 'top' of this triangular field. Pass through the gateway here and follow the hedgelines on your left, which soon turn right, and walk to the far left-hand corner of this field.

3 Go through the gate here and turn left to follow the hedgeline on your left through this field and the next. At the end of this second field, the path turns right along the hedgeline and then, after a few yards, left to pass through a gateway into the next field. The path then crosses this field to a gateway on the far side. Through this it then follows the field boundary on your left soon to run alongside a small wood. Just past the end of the wood

HUMBER COURT & CHURCH

The farmhouse dates from the 17th century and was extended and refronted in the mid 19th century. It is largely built of sandstone rubble with ashlar dressings around door and window openings. The earliest part of the church is the chancel, which dates from the 12th century. The nave and tower date from the 13th century, and the timber porch from the 14th century.

it passes through another gateway and follows the track ahead alongside another field boundary and then across grassland. Here it soon passes the remnants of a walled garden on your right.

Continue ahead on this track, soon passing above the large red brick house called Buckland and entering a straggling farmyard.

4 Past the house and several of the buildings (but about 100 yards before you reach some farm cottages), turn right to pass between some smaller farm buildings and walk down a track to a gate into a field to the right of a stone wall. Once in the field beyond this gate, turn slightly right and aim for the corner of another field that juts into the one you're in from the left. (You'll get better views of Buckland off to your right at this point.) Once at this corner of the field, follow the hedgeline on your left to a gate into the field beyond. Here the path drops downhill to the far right-hand corner of the field. (Keep to the right of the single tree that stands in the field.)

5 Now cross the bridge across the Holly Brook. Here the path briefly turns into a track to lead you to a gate into the field on the other side of the brook. Ignore any signs for another path that heads off to the left at this point. Once in this field, the path heads for a point on the hedgerow on the left-hand side as it heads uphill that is roughly adjacent to the second free-standing oak in the field. If crops are obstructing the way, or if the farmer has left a headland path round the edge of the field, you might be advised to follow the hedgelines round on your left to reach this point. By whichever route you reach it, once you have passed the second oak, ignoring a stile in the hedgerow almost adjacent to it, follow the hedgeline a bit further, and when it has swung a little to the left, keep an eye out for another stile in the hedgerow. Cross this, and turn right to join a track which promptly leads out of the field you're now in. Follow this track, which keeps pretty well straight ahead, ignoring all turns to right or left, and it will lead you down to the crossroads in Risbury Cross. Turn left to return to where you parked.

field. Here the path shadows the brook in a gentle arc to the right, eventually aiming for a small timber-framed cottage. In front of this you will come to a gate which you go through to join a road.

6 Turn left on this and almost immediately right over the stile into the field adjacent to the cottage, following that house's boundary along to a bridge over a stream. From here you walk along the banks of the river Teme on your left to another footbridge, which you cross to reach Little Hereford church.

7 To return to Brimfield, recross the footbridge over the Teme, and then walk across the field on the line of the bridge, and up the bank on the far side, at the top of which you will find an opening into an orchard. (When last walking the route a hurdle had replaced a stile at this point.). It can be a little

LITTLE HEREFORD CHURCH & CASTLE

Little Hereford is so named as the parish was 'peculiar' to the canons of Hereford Cathedral, and so was outside the bishop's jurisdiction. The church has an unusual arrangement of a chancel arch with a rood loft (which still survives) above it. The archway that would have once held an altar with a cross suspended above it is now blocked in but a stone cross has been set in the framed space. The altar was dedicated to the Virgin Mary and the piscina, in which the holy vessels for use at the altar were washed, remains to the right of the arch with the letters B.B. probably standing for Beata Beatissima, meaning 'Blessed, the most blessed'. In the chancel are two tomb recesses in the Decorated style, and a set of sedilia (recessed seats for priests).

Earthworks to the north and east of the church, between it and the river, mark the site of a possible castle. The mound between the footbridge and the church might be the remains of a motte. If this is the site of the castle, and the Normans often placed church and castle in close conjunction, it was where King Stephen came with an army in 1139 and again in 1140 from Worcester on his way to do battle with forces in Hereford supporting Matilda, and where he sought negotiations with the Mortimers and the lords of neighbouring castles to bolster his support in the area. Alternatively, because the earthworks to the east of the church are quite extensive, more than would be expected at a minor castle site, it may be that they represent a camp that King Stephen erected as he used Little Hereford as his base. To add further confusion, the humps and bumps may represent the site of a house that belonged to the Delamere family which is said to have been located between the church and the river. In c.1521 the house was abandoned and a new residence was built at Bleathwood.

difficult to see the path up the bank, especially when the grass is long, but you need to head straight up the bank (rather than taking the lower path that slants across it further along); the opening in the hedge at the top is about 100 yards from the right-hand end of the hedge. Cross the orchard between the lines of trees to a gate out onto a road.

8 Cross the road and follow the bridleway that initially follows the field boundary on your left, then passes through a gate that faces you in a corner of the field to follow the field boundary now on your right, all the while heading uphill on the same line. You will come to a gate into the next field, through which you keep following the field boundary on your right. When the boundary turns sharp right, keep on straight ahead across the field for some 200 yards to pick up the field boundary again on your right and carry on to the corner of the field where you meet a road.

9 Turn right on the road and follow it along as it makes a series of right- and left-hand bends as it passes between various farms, including Upton Court, drops down to cross a stream and then rises to a T-junction.

10 Turn left here. After you pass a house on the right-hand side, turn right up the no-through road (signposted Middleton Wood) that runs alongside some red brick farm buildings. Where the road bends to the left just beyond these, continue ahead to enter a field by a wide gravel track, then follow the hedge on your right. After about 50 yards you will reach a gap in the hedge. Go through this, cross the bridge, then head across the next field to the far left-hand corner, a point which is to the immediate right of a small copse. Cross the stile and bridge here, then head across the next field aiming directly at the chimneys and Dutch gables of Nun Upton (the house is to the left of the farm buildings). If the path is obstructed by crops, walk round the edge of the field.

11 Cross the stile by the house into a small grassy yard, in which you turn right to cross and then turn left to leave

NUN UPTON

Nun Upton was built in the 16th century, partially clad in brick in the late 17th century and restored in the early 20th century, which included rebuilding the timber-framed porch. At one time it was the property of Limebrook nunnery (see p.56), hence the first word of the house's name. At the Dissolution it was bought by Richard Andrews, and it passed from him to the branch of the Cornewall family of Berrington, whose heiress married Thomas Pitt c.1760. The only son of their marriage, Mr Cornewall Pitt, was declared a lunatic and the property was held in trust for him.

by a gate to reach a tarmacked drive. Keep ahead on this for a few yards, then turn left to walk along the drive that leads past the house on your left, followed by a small stone building, to enter a field. Here the path turns half-right to shadow the hedgeline on your right to reach a gap in a line of trees just over the crest of the hill. Here you will join a path that emerges from the woodland on your right, turning left on the path that heads along the edge of the hill through the mature trees standing in the field to a stile that leads into another block of woodland. Cross this, and emerge into another field. Keep following the fenceline on your right, (you may need to follow tramlines), essentially walking along the edge of the ridge, and at the corner of the field, follow the footpath that keeps straight on (it can be overgrown in summer), dropping down into a little gully and rising up the other side to enter another field. Keep following the fenceline on your right to the far end of this field, where you pass out by a stile, to immediately cross a second stile on your right.

Head straight down the hillside, in due course aiming for a stile very close to a right-angled bend in the field boundary at the bottom of the hill. Cross this stile and then a plank bridge to enter the next field. Now follow the field boundary on your right down to another stile and footbridge. Over these bear slightly left and follow the line of an old and now straggly hedge to another stile. Once over this the path turns slightly to the right to technically cross a corner of this field towards a pair of large oaks,

but, depending upon the crop growing in the field, you might find it easier to walk around the edge of the field to this point. However reached, once near the oaks, simply keep following the field boundary on your right. At the far end of the field cross a stile and then pass alongside a red-brick building followed by a house. Cross another stile into the next field and follow the field boundary on your right to another stile and bridge to enter a further field. Keep following the field boundary on your right and pass another house to leave the field by a stile.

⓬ Cross the lane you find here, passing over another stile into the field on the far side. Now follow the field boundary on your left and this will soon lead you down to another stile that you cross as you approach the church and churchyard at Brimfield. Follow the churchyard wall around on your left and this will lead you back to the stile that you crossed near the start of the walk. Recross this and carry on down the lane ahead to return to the Roebuck.

Walk 13
Croft Ambrey

5.75 miles, largely on forest tracks, minor roads and paths across fields, with one sharp ascent and one sharp descent. Some stiles. Includes a major hillfort.

This walk starts from the Riverside Inn at Aymestrey, where you can park so long as you take sustenance at the pub before or after your walk (GR 425 654).

1 From the inn, cross the bridge. Just before you reach the minor road on your left, take the signposted footpath on the other side of the road, passing through gates immediately to the left of a cottage. Follow the track through the field ahead, initially alongside the boundary of the cottage's garden and keep following the track until you reach a stile and gate. Once through this, turn

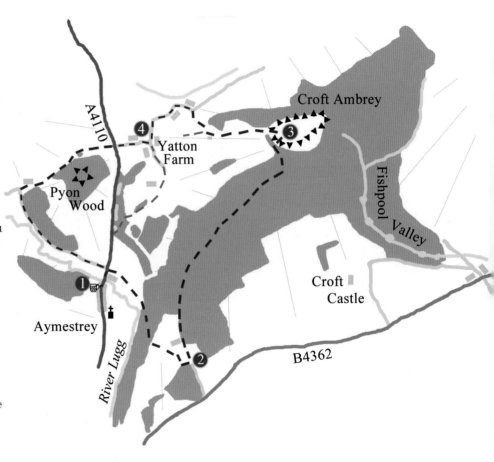

half-right to aim for a stile roughly half-way along a fence that runs from the foot of the hill ahead down to the river. Cross this stile, then head for the foot of the hill at the far top corner of the next field, passing to the left of a slightly sunken area within the field.

Once over the stile here, take the path that leads up the hillside, initially up steps. It crosses a track that slopes downhill from left to right, and thereafter takes a gently weaving course up the hillside, to cross a stile (with dog gate) and emerge into a field at the top. Once in this field, head directly away from the woodland from which you've just emerged to a stile in the field boundary opposite. Cross this, and then head across the next field to a stile in the far left-hand corner. Cross a pair of stiles at this field boundary, and then follow the fenceline on your left downhill, passing out of the field by a field gate on your left in the bottom corner, and then walking down a short length of track to join a tarmacked lane.

2 Turn left on this lane. It soon becomes a gravelled track as it passes a house on the left and then you go through a pedestrian gate and straight ahead, entering woodland on each side. Keep on this track for about a mile, it gently taking you uphill. At the crest, you'll come to a crossroads of paths. Turn left here (following the blue arrow), and follow the track which will lead you to a stile and field gate just below the ramparts of Croft Ambrey. Once over the stile, or through the gate, take the path

round the left of the ramparts, cross the stile and follow the track that curls into the hillfort.

③ When exploring the hillfort (quite a large space), bear in mind that you will be leaving it by crossing a stile to the left of the point where you entered it. You can take any one of a number of small paths that lead towards this north-west corner of the hillfort, where the stile will lead you out onto a spur of the hillside. Here you have views across the old Wigmore lake, with the possibility of spotting Wigmore Castle on the hill above the village when trees are bereft of leaves. (The lake which filled the shallow basin from where you're standing across to Wigmore was formed by glacial meltwater that was blocked from flowing southwards through the gap in the hills towards where Aymestrey now stands by glacial moraine. Eventually the pressure of the water forced a way out northwards, creating the Downton gorge; see Walk 14.) The Long Mynd can be seen to the right, and ahead, across the aptly named Wigmore Rolls, is the thimble-like shape of The Whimble in Radnor Forest. Half-left is the long line of the Black Mountains on the skyline.

The path you want from here is that which runs almost due west directly down the spur. This will lead you to a gate (near a cottage) through which you pass; then follow the sunken path as it bends right and continues downhill to meet a road.

slightly left to go straight across the field through some bracken and trees to enter the woodland via a gate. The path now slants up across the hillside (ignore a path off to the right shortly after entering the wood) to emerge at the top of the woodland at a choice of gate or stile. In the field you turn half-right to head towards a group of large trees on the crest of the slope where it is crossed by a fence. As you reach this fence near the group of trees you will see a slightly sunken track alongside the fence, and you want to follow this to a gate near the corner of the field which you go through. From slightly beyond this point you should be able to see Downton Castle (especially in winter) on the far side of the river Teme, which is in the valley below you.

The path initially follows this track, but after about 200 yards bears left downhill, aiming just to the right of an oak that stands inside the bottom of the field. Cross the stile here into some heathland and thence descend to meet another track. Turn right on this track and pass through a short section of woodland to emerge in the corner of a large field on your left. The footpath heads diagonally across this field towards the far corner, but the farmer may not have reinstated the footpath after agricultural activity. If this is the case, you can follow tramlines, walk round the edge of the field, or stay on the track and follow it along one side of the field, then, at the end of the field, turn left on another track to walk down to reach the field's far corner.

3 From the field's far corner you take the track that heads towards Downton Castle, soon entering the Downton Gorge Nature Reserve. The track soon heads through some woodland and then over a bridge across the Teme, past ruins of houses, a cave (only really visible in winter), then bends right along the bottom of the slope in front of Downton Castle. Follow this track as it rises gently uphill below the castle.

4 Just before the track swings left beyond Downton Castle, watch for the waymarking sign on a post on the right, and follow the indicated footpath down to a footpath gate near a part timber-framed house. Go through the gate and turn left on the house's driveway, then right at

DOWNTON GORGE NATURE RESERVE

The woodland's rare trees include large-leaved lime, small-leaved-lime and sessile oak. There is extensive pollarding, notably of oaks and limes, from charcoal-making in years gone by. Wild service trees are to be found. The cliffs of the gorge support rare plants such as wood fescue and rock stonecrop, and they are also important for ferns. The reserve is rich in mosses and lichens, some of which are rare and only associated with ancient wood pasture. There are polecats, otters and a long-haired species of fallow deer only found in this area of Britain. The underlying geology produces both limey and acidic soils in different parts of the reserve, and contains a variety of fossils.

DOWNTON CASTLE

The Downton estate was acquired in the early 1700s by Richard Knight, a wealthy ironmaster of Madeley, Shropshire, to provide charcoal for his expanding iron smelting business. In around 1764 the estate passed to his grandson, Richard Payne Knight, an antiquarian and artistic theorist who had spent time in Italy on the Grand Tour. He had become passionate about the Picturesque movement, which felt that the wildness of nature, especially craggy rocks and turbulent rivers, should be revered and where possible enhanced by romantic ruins. Knight duly designed an asymmetrical house in the Picturesque style, the building that remains in its essential details to this day. He also erected a number of follies in the grounds, including Roman baths and a cave with windows cut out of the rock. In 1780 he became MP for Leominster, and from 1784 to 1806 sat for Ludlow.

In 1839, Charles Greville wrote in his diary for 26 June: 'I rode to Downton Castle on Monday, a gimcrack castle and bad house, built by Payne Knight, an epicurean philosopher, who after building the castle went and lived in a lodge or cottage in the park: there he died, not without suspicion of having put an end to himself, which would have been fully conformable to his notions. He was a sensualist in all ways, but a great and self-educated scholar. His property is now in Chancery, because he chose to make his own will. The prospect from the windows is beautiful, and the walk through the wood, overhanging the river Teme, surpasses anything I have ever seen of the kind.'

Children's writer Malcolm Saville used Downton Castle as a basis for Bringewood Manor in his 1958 Lone Pine adventure *The Secret of the Gorge*. Downton Gorge is now leased to English Nature as a National Nature Reserve.

DOWNTON IRONWORKS

The river Teme flowing through Downton Gorge produced enough power to work both a furnace to produce pig iron (created from ore that largely came from the Clee Hills) and a forge to refine it into wrought iron. The business began in 1584; as it developed, more power was needed and the works began to consume charcoal voraciously. Richard Knight took a lease on the ironworks in 1698, and by 1717 the forge was producing 340 tons of pig iron a year. In 1723 Knight acquired the freehold of extensive areas of woodland around the iron-works, presumably to help make sufficient charcoal. In the 1730s Edward Knight, Richard's son, built a tinplate rolling mill at Bringewood. It needed water to clean and power it, a supply of wrought iron and a plentiful and cheap fuel supply. The Seven Years' War in the 1750s boosted demand, but costs rose during the 1760s and the mill was closed in the mid 1770s. By 1779 only the forge continued to work and in 1783 Richard Payne Knight took over ownership and invested in the iron-works to keep it productive. The ironworks now comprised three fineries (where pig iron was converted to rough wrought iron) and one chafery which further shaped and purified the iron. It was fuelled by coal from the mid 1750s, but had ceased production by 1815 as large-scale manufacture elsewhere made production at Bringewood uneconomic. At its height, the complex included three bellows and two hammers each powered by a waterwheel, a particularly large waterwheel powering the blowing tubs at the furnace and five waterwheels at the rolling and slitting mills.

the junction of driveways quickly reached. As you reach the end of the stone-built cottage on your right, the path leaves the driveway and passes through a field gate. Turn left to shadow the river, the path initially keeping to the bottom of the bank on your left and soon gaining a more visible form. Keep to it till you reach the next bridge.

5 Once up the embankment and onto the lane that crosses the bridge, turn left away from the bridge. When the lane forks, take the branch to the left that passes in front of a pair of semi-detached cottages. Immediately past the cottages, take the footpath to the right, which presently enters a field by a stile. The path crosses this field by slightly diverging from the fence and field boundary on the right, passing some 20 yards to the left of a large single oak in the field, and leaves by a stile in a dip onto a minor road. (The farmer does reinstate the path, but if it looks difficult to walk you could return to the road junction near the cottages, turn left and reach the minor road that way.)

6 Turn left on the minor road which crosses Stone Brook with its evidence of water mills. Further on it passes the 'new' Downton church of St Giles built in 1861 to the design of Pountney Smith. Stay on this road, ignoring all turnings to the right, and turning left when you come to a T-junction. Cross the bridge over the Teme, then take the next lane left to return to your vehicle, visiting Burrington church en route if you wish.

101

BURRINGTON CHURCH

The present church dates from 1855-64. It is unusually dedicated to St George, though there was a fashion for such dedications in the Victorian era. The feature that distinguishes this church from many is the collection of cast iron grave slabs currently located outside the east end of the church (they used to be in the chancel). They span burials from 1619 to 1754, some of them of members of the Knight family (see p.99), and were made in the forges of Bringewood.

Walk 15
Leintwardine

5 miles, largely on tracks and minor roads with a few field edge paths (largely grassland). No stiles. Includes an historic inn, Roman town planning, and a church.

From the A4113, turn into the village and park near the Sun Inn (GR 405 737).

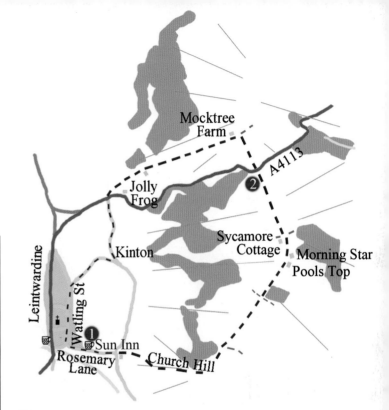

THE SUN INN, LEINTWARDINE

The Sun Inn began life as a simple beer house (selling only beer brewed on the premises) in 1876 under William Jones, who seems also to have been a tailor. By 1903 it was selling cider as well, and beer and cider was all it sold for decades afterwards. In the 1970s it was run by Charles Lane and his spinster sister Flossie. The inn had no bar as such, beer and cider being brought out in glasses from the back of the house to a room at the front with two long tables. After Charles died, Flossie continued running it till her death in June 2009. The pub was to be sold at auction, but after a national media campaign Sun regular Gary Seymour and Nick Davis of Hobson's Brewery were able to acquire the inn. They are keeping the front 'parlour bar' as close as possible to the style it had when Flossie was there, and have added a single-storey rear extension that provides a bar and more space.

---

❶ With your back to the entrance to the Sun, turn left and walk along the road. When you reach a T-junction, turn left towards Kinton, then cross the road and go through a metal footpath gate to follow a path steeply straight uphill. You cross a grassy track which you soon meet for a second time, when you turn left onto it. The

track will lead you round the left-hand side of an old quarry, before bending to the right to pass through part of it. Follow the track into the next field and after about 80 yards stay on the track as it bends right and immediately left through the line of the field boundary to carry on uphill where it gains a hedge to its left and a fence to its right.

Continue on the track uphill as it largely curves in a shallow arc to the left, it soon losing any boundary to its left, gaining a hedge to its right, passing a farm building to its left and gaining a gravelled surface. Ignore all signs of paths to right or left together with any tracks to right or left. Just beyond one crossroads of tracks you immediately pass a small wood on the right. As the track nears the houses of Pools Top followed by Morning Star, it turns more decidedly to the left, and then continues to rise up the hillside to reach Sycamore Cottage on the left-hand side. Just beyond this cottage you reach a tarmacked lane on which you turn left (ignoring another track that also branches off to the left) to follow the lane uphill for a short while, then downhill to meet the main road.

2 Cross the main road to follow a lane that leads straight ahead. At the end of the field on your left it meets a wide track, on which you turn left to pass in front of a stone-built house, shortly followed by a second house. Stay on this track which leads gently downhill, often with a stony surface, later passing a house on your left and gaining a tarmacked surface as it serves as the access lane for a number of houses. Keep on this lane which will meet the main road which you cross to take the minor road on its far side. Follow this downhill through cuttings and past Kinton Farm to a T-junction at which you turn right. Follow the road as it bends left and in due course reach another T-junction. Turn left here onto Watling Street and pass the church on the right, which you might choose to visit. The walk continues down Watling Street, turning left at the bottom to return to the Sun.

ROMAN LEINTWARDINE

Leintwardine lies on the edge of the plain at the confluence of the rivers Clun and Teme, and possibly at the border between the territories of two Celtic tribes, the Cornovii and the Dobunni. The site was one of those earmarked by the Romans for military forts or settlements along the road known as Watling Street West, which they built along the length of the Welsh border from Chepstow via Caerwent to Chester, Leintwardine lying almost halfway between *Magnis* (the forerunner of Hereford) and *Viroconium* (Wroxeter). Two temporary marching camps were established at Walford and Brampton Bryan to the south-west, followed by a cavalry fort at Jay Lane to the north-east, two successive cavalry forts at Buckton to the west, and a civilian settlement at Leintwardine. There is some debate over the Roman name for this settlement. Whilst there is agreement that it was later known as *Bravonium*, was it known earlier as *Branogenium* or was that the name of one of the forts in the area? In the 'Antonine Itinerary', *Branogenium* is given as one of the stopping places for the imperial messenger service. Excavations in Leintwardine have revealed evidence of a bathhouse near the river and an inn, likely requirements for a messenger in need of refreshment.

The settlement was laid out to a regular 'playing card' shape, suggesting that its surveyors had at least been trained in the Roman army. The A4113 bisects the Roman town and follows the line of the original Watling Street, whilst the current Watling Street (which parallels the A4113 to the east) runs along the line of the ditch outside the Roman settlement. This can be seen in the gardens of the houses to its west, which rise steeply over the town's rampart. The rampart was not in fact built when the settlement was initially constructed *circa* 80-90 AD; it was constructed around 170 AD, it is believed as a result of upheaval in Britain during a time of civil war in the Empire that was eventually settled by Septimus Severus in the 190s. (Severus was to die in York in 211 after an unsuccessful attempt to incorporate what was to become Scotland into the Roman Empire.)

LEINTWARDINE CHURCH

In Saxon days Leintwardine was the centre of a hundred that covered parts of present day Herefordshire, Shropshire and Radnorshire. By the time of the Domesday Survey it had passed into the hands of the Mortimers who, around a hundred years later, gave the church to their abbey at Wigmore. The building dates essentially from the 13th and 14th centuries, with traces of earlier Norman work, and has south and north aisles, as well as a chancel with a north chapel. The chancel and chapel have a higher floor level than the rest of the church, it is believed because they were erected on the remains of a building dating from the Roman settlement. The stalls in the chancel are believed to have come from Wigmore Abbey and contain misericords with the usual rich mixture of subjects, and one more unusual one: a recently carved misericord shows the parlour bar of the Sun Inn.

There is a memorial in the north chapel to General Sir Banastre Tarleton who, having gambled away his inheritance, led an irregular force during the American War of Independence (as a Lt Colonel) in which he gained the soubriquet 'Bloody Tarleton'. Returning to England, he became an MP for Liverpool, was a staunch supporter of the slave trade and eventually retired to Leintwardine where he died in 1833. In the Sun Inn you can see a copy of the portrait of Tarleton by Joshua Reynolds, the original of which hangs in the National Gallery.

slightly to the right and leaves the field via a stile in its far corner. The path now passes between a hedge on your left and a fence on your right and above a large pond, to reach a gate into another field. Here the path follows the line of the fence on your left, and in due course turns into a track which will lead you past some farm buildings on your left to a concrete farm access road. Turn right on this and it becomes the lane on which you started the walk.

5 For a walk around Bromyard, when you reach the end of the lane, continue ahead, passing the timber-framed Tower House on your right. Cross the A44 by the underpass and continue down Pump Street, past the site of the old tanyard on your right to the junction with High and Broad Street. Turn right and walk up to the square, which you cross diagonally. Cross the street on the far side and turn left into Church Street. Walk along this and turn left into the churchyard of St Peter's church.

6 Having visited the church, turn right out of the door and leave the churchyard by the gateway ahead. Turn left along Church Lane, with two terraces of Victorian houses on your right. At the entrance to a car park on your left, go into the car park and walk through the metal gates immediately on your right. Walk through the garden, then leave it near Bromyard Public Hall by a stone-pillared gateway. Cross Rowberry Street, then walk past the almshouses (pictured middle above) and take the first left down the High Street to the Falcon Hotel. Turn right here, back along Pump Street, to return to the Tower House.

Walk 17
Thornbury & Wacton

5.25 miles on minor roads, paths (many of them across pasture land) and some tracks with few stiles. Includes a church, a castle site, an old manor house, a disused railway line and a hillfort. This is a revised walk from the version included in the earlier edition of the book, as, on the footpaths leading from Great Wacton towards Thornbury hillfort, one footbridge had been destroyed and it was unclear when it would be replaced and, secondly, one crossing between fields had become extremely overgrown. Unfortunately it now means that you need to retrace your steps for part of the walk. It's nevertheless a very pleasant walk.

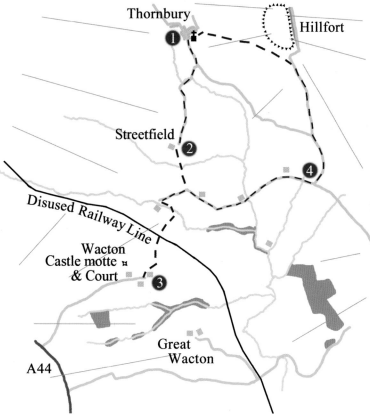

Park in Thornbury near St Anna's church. There are a couple of parking places on the lane that leads to the church (GR 623 597).

❶ After visiting the church, walk back down to the road and turn left. Take the first minor road off to the right (signposted Streetfield) in a few hundred yards. In due course this will come to an end at Streetfield farm.

❷ Here, keep to the track which follows the line of the minor road, passing to the left of the farm. This dips down and then rises to meet another minor road. Turn right on

THORNBURY CHURCH (St Anna's)
There is a fine blocked Norman doorway in the north wall of the nave, and a Norman font inside the church. The nave was built in the 12th century, the massive tower dates from the Early English period in the 13th century, and Frederick Kempson rebuilt the chancel in 1865.

this and you will drop down to a cattle grid. Immediately across this go through the gate on the left signed Orchard Place and Butterley Brook, then immediately turn left to take a bridleway through some woodland, following a stream on your right. The bridleway passes through one gate and then another, to enter a large field. Turn right along the field boundary; then the path cuts across the corner of the field, heading for a tunnel beneath the old railway line (possibly obscured by foliage in summer). Once you are through the tunnel, the path turns slightly left to cross the next field to the field boundary on the far side, in front of which it turns right. As you cross the field, you should be able to see the remnants of the motte of Wacton Castle in the next field over to your right (see photo above). When you reach the end of the field, go through the footpath gate found between two field

WACTON CASTLE, COURT & CHURCH

Wacton Court dates from the early 17th century, though it has been partially rebuilt since, including the 18th-century brick-faced south wing. The moat originally surrounded the building, and further enclosures lie to the east and north. To the north also lies an oval motte with the remains of a moat on the west. Buried foundations suggest that the motte supported a round tower with a side projection, possibly a gatehouse. A line of loose stone running from the motte to the surviving arm of the moat around Wacton Court shows up after ploughing or in dry conditions as yellowing in the crop and indicates the line of a curtain wall. Possible defences on the east of the site have been obscured by farm buildings (since demolished) and more recent landscaping. Pieces of stone have been discovered on the site with diagonal tooling and fragments of what appear to be late 13th-century to early 14th-century windows, which could have come from either the castle or the church, largely demolished in 1881 with the remaining traces of its walls recently knocked down. The church would have been built roughly at the same time as the castle, in usual Norman fashion, and provided for the inhabitants of the settlement that would have formed under the castle's protection.

gates to join a track which you follow. In due course this becomes a minor road; walk along it to see Wacton Court and its moat.

WALL HILLS, THORNBURY

A single massive rampart and deep ditch enclose an oval area of about 23 acres, and probably date from the early Iron Age. Even now the rampart rises as high as 12 feet above the inner level and 40 feet above the bottom of the outer ditch, which has largely been filled in except on the northern side. There are currently four entrances, but only two are original, one on the south-east where the rampart is both turned inwards and projected outwards, so forming an entrance passage, and one at the northern end of the western side, which has suffered subsequent damage. There are remains of field terraces or lynchets to the south-west and the east. Duncumb in 1822 recorded that ditches extended for some considerable distance in various directions (towards Netherwood, Kyre Common and Collington) outwards from the hillfort. No traces of dwellings have yet been found inside the hillfort, though two cannon balls have!

To the south-east of the hillfort, most notably in the area now covered by Edwyn Wood (out of sight on the walk, being on the downside of the hill slope), many of the remaining field boundaries form long parallel lines, a pattern interrupted by the hillfort itself. It's possible, therefore, that the origins of the modern field pattern date back to the Bronze Age.

5 Once in the woodland, follow the path ahead, keeping right at the first two junctions to then pass alongside a small car park to your right. Keep to what becomes a large track as it starts to drop downhill, but take the first path off to the right. This passes close to a cottage on the right to then meet a track on which you turn right and immediately left onto a path that heads down some steps. Further downhill the path becomes a wide track, which bends to the right and which you follow downhill to meet a crossroads of tracks and paths. Go straight over the 'crossroads' to take a path down to a stream where there is a sculpture of a horse; this seems to be the one remaining element of what had been a sculpture trail.

The path crosses a stream by a bridge to reach a T-junction of paths, where you turn left. You now follow the stream on your left for several hundred yards, keeping an eye out for a short length of path that leads down to a track that crosses the stream, for this you want to take! Once you've found the path, headed down it and reached the track, turn left to cross the stream by a concrete bridge and then immediately right up a path which climbs the hillside with the help of several steps. When you reach a T-junction of paths, turn right and follow this along to where it makes a 'crossroads' of paths and tracks near a small lake.

Turn right and cross the lake's 'dam', to leave the woodland by a gate. Here walk uphill for about 20 yards towards a large oak ahead of you, in front of which you'll find a grassy track. Take this and follow it as it slants up and across the hillside to a block of woodland.

BROCKHAMPTON

In the 1200s the manor belonged to the aptly named de Brockhamptons. They sold it in 1283 to Robert de Furches, but it returned to the ownership of a descendant of the Brockhamptons, John Domulton, in 1403. John is generally thought to have been the builder of Brockhampton Court, which still stands on the moated site. The timber-framed gatehouse was added in the late 15th or early 16th century. The manor passed through the Habingtons to the Barneby family (by marriage) and thence, in 1726, to Richard Lutley, a nephew of the Barnebys. He commissioned Thomas Farnolls Pritchard to build a new mansion, Brockhampton House, in parkland to the south, and the old building was relegated to the role of a farmhouse, a first floor being inserted into the great hall. The building became derelict, but was restored in 1871 and then bequeathed with the 1,680-acre Brockhampton estate to the National Trust in 1946. An earthwork survey carried out in 2003 indicated that the original moat was larger than the present one. It also showed that a west wing once existed, meaning that the house conformed to the usual H-plan for a hall house: central hall with a solar, or living, wing for the lord and lady of the manor, and a service wing on the far side of the hall, so keeping the dangerous kitchens, from which fire might spread, away from the living quarters.

The chapel, of which only the walls remain, dates from the 12th century and lies outside the moat that encircles the house. At this date the moated site was presumably protected by a drawbridge and gatehouse.

6 Cross the stile here and follow the track ahead through the woodland and alongside a mossy wall. Bear left at a junction of paths and leave the woodland by a gate on the far side. Walk up to the tarmacked lane. (Here, you can walk down the lane on the right to Brockhampton Court, returning the same way.) The walk continues by going ahead uphill on the tarmacked lane and keeping straight on where it splits at a point where exit signs for drivers point left by the church. (At this junction there has sometimes been a National Trust tea room.) About 100 yards after this split, the tarmacked lane bends to the right; here, keep straight ahead on a track that leads gently uphill to a gate. Go through this gate and keep following the track between fields till you reach a farm. Here you meet a gravel track on which you turn right and so pass round to the right of all the farm buildings. The track then reverts to an earthen surface and when you reach a gate across the track, go through it and keep following the hedge on your left. You soon pass above a wood on your right to reach a pond called the Shepherd's Pool on your left. Beyond this pond the path passes through a small gate to continue in the same direction

but now following a thin strip of woodland on your right. Beyond the field you pass a derelict cottage on your left to emerge via a small gate back onto Bromyard Downs. Turn left and head downhill to return to the layby.

Walk 19
Acton Beauchamp

4 miles, largely on paths across and along field edges, minor roads and tracks. A few stiles. Includes a church.

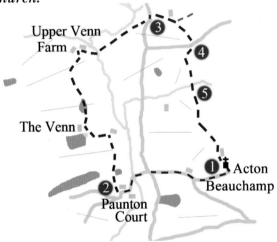

Park on the no-through lane that leads to the church (GR 680 503).

1 Walk back down the lane and turn right when you reach the road. Go over the crossroads reached in about a quarter of a mile, after which the road jinks left and then right to pass through the buildings of Paunton Court.

2 Just beyond the buildings, take the signposted footpath (also signposted to The Farm) off to the right down a wide track. Keep straight ahead on this and cross a pair of driveways to follow a metalled lane along the foot of the sloping ground on your left. The lane leads to The Venn, a partially timber-framed farmhouse with two oast houses and a range of barns. When you reach the cattlegrid at the entrance to the farm complex, the path keeps to the right to go through a footpath gate and then follows the field boundary on your left. At the end of this field (a hopyard in 2021) you go through a strip of woodland to reach another footpath gate.

Go through this gate and then follow the field boundary on your left, following it round to the left and uphill for about 20 yards. The path then turns right to cross the field, keeping the large single trees in the field to your right. Go through the field gate on the far side of the field, then turn half right and walk down to a gateway in a hedge to the right of the farm buildings (of Upper Venn Farm) ahead. Once through this gateway, turn left towards the buildings and follow the field boundary round to pick up the lane that serves the farm. Turn right on this and follow it down to the road.

3 Turn left on the road and after a few yards, and just before another farm lane, turn right onto a footpath which leads through a corner of field to then follow a field boundary on your left. Ignore the stile that appears

straight ahead of you, and bear right to continue to follow the field boundary on your left. About 100 yards beyond the stile just mentioned you will come to a footbridge on your left, which you cross into the field beyond. Aim slightly to the left of the telegraph pole that is almost at the top of the rise in the middle of the field, and as you reach this you should spot the stile exit in the hedgerow beyond, just to the left of another telegraph pole.

4 Once over the stile and on the road turn right and almost immediately left through one gateway, then go through a second on the right to enter a field. Follow the hedgeline on your right to the next field gateway, and once through this, turn left and directly downhill, following the hedgeline on your left. When this makes a sharp left turn, keep going straight ahead for a few more yards to a lip in the slope, then turn slightly to the right and keep going downhill – you should be able to make out a bridge across the stream in the valley bottom towards which you want to head.

5 Cross the bridge and go up the bank on the far side to enter the next field by a small gate. Go through the gateway on your right and then up the slope, with your back to the stream and a hedge on your left. At the top of the field cross a stile and go straight across the next field on the same line that you've just been walking to reach another stile. Over this, turn half-left to cross the next field, aiming for the junction between a hedge running up the hillside from the right and a taller stand of trees coming over the hill from the left. Here you will find another stile, which you cross and then follow the field boundary on your right towards a house. As you approach this you will come to a stile on your right which you cross, to then follow the boundary of the house's grounds on your left, going past the house to reach a stile followed by a small gate that will lead you into the churchyard of Acton Beauchamp. From the church, walk down the path from the south door to the lane to return to your vehicle.

ACTON BEAUCHAMP CHURCH

The tower is medieval; the rest of the church was rebuilt in the Georgian style in 1819 and still retains its Georgian ambience. The lintel to the south doorway to the tower is made from an Anglo-Saxon cross-shaft dating, probably, from the 9th century. It is possible that this comes from a Saxon monastery that existed somewhere in the vicinity, for Aethelbald, king of Mercia from 716 to 757, granted 3 hides of land at Acton Beauchamp to Buca for a religious community. Certainly the presence of the yew tree indicates an ancient religious site. (Another association with trees is that the name Acton means a settlement by oak trees, with which the area is dotted.) By 972 any monastic foundation in the area would appear to have been subsumed into that of Pershore, for King Edgar confirmed the grant of the 3 hides to Pershore monastery. However, to add further confusion, by the time of the Domesday Survey, when the land area had grown to 6 hides, it was held by one Urso from Odo, the bishop of Bayeux, half-brother of William the Conqueror, who seems to have obtained the land from the monks of Evesham.

Look closely at the south door to the church, which is a reset Norman doorway: the numbers incised in the stones to aid their ordering in the rebuild can be seen, and there is a reconsecration cross on the right-hand jamb.

4 Ledbury
& the Malverns

LEDBURY

The settlement began its life around a minster church founded probably in the 700s to minister to the surrounding part of the recently created Hereford Diocese. As with most minster churches, a market was soon established just outside the gateway to the church, and this spread down what became Church Lane. At that time the main east/west route was along Bye Street and then up Back Lane, the narrow lane that runs more or less parallel to Church Lane, just to its north. It wasn't until the coming of the turnpikes in the 1700s that the current route of more gentle pitch for carriage traffic was created past Ledbury Park.

It was probably during the reign of Henry I that the settlement gained its first charter, which granted it the right to have burgesses (freemen who paid an annual rent to the Church and governed themselves in many matters). A new market place, of the traditional wedge shape favoured by the Normans, was laid out at the bottom of Church Lane, off which burgage plots were laid out. In Ledbury these varied in width but were all about 200 feet (or 12 perches in medieval terms) in depth. The ground floor often had a shop at the front with work space to the rear, and living space on the floor or floors above. Over time some of the burgage plots were acquired by neighbours to form larger frontages, adding even greater variety to the widths of properties. But they all needed easy access to the rear of their premises without having to go through the shop and workspaces, so some created alleyways for this purpose, and sometimes neighbours combined to share an alleyway. Many of these remain and some now lead to small courtyards off which other houses, shops and businesses can be found.

Ledbury found itself on the front line during the English Civil War, with Parliamentarian forces sometimes present in the town from their base in Gloucester, and on other occasions Royalist troops from Hereford or further afield. In 1644 Colonel Massey, the Parliamentarian governor of Gloucester, then based in Ledbury, found himself under a surprise attack from a force led by Prince Rupert. It was one of the few occasions in the war when Massey was worsted, and a story has it that each of the commanders had a horse shot under him.

These days Ledbury is home to an annual poetry festival, building on a poetic tradition that includes Langland (see p.167), Elizabeth Barrett Browning (see p.158) and John Masefield. Masefield was born in the town in 1878 and was Poet Laureate from 1930 until his death in 1967. Many of his poems and stories about the English countryside are based on his recollections of life in and around Ledbury.

Walk 20
Ledbury

2.5 miles, largely on roads, disused railway track, woodland paths and tracks, and field edge paths. Few stiles. Includes parts of Ledbury including the Market Hall and church, as well as ancient woodland above the town.

1 From the bottom of Church Lane, turn left and walk up the High Street, with the Market Hall on your right, to the crossroads. Keep an eye out, whilst on this part of the walk, for the various alleyways that lead off between properties. Cross the High Street at Ledbury Park, and turn right back down it.

You will pass the Feathers Inn, which was built in 1570 at the start of a great period of rebuilding in Ledbury that lasted till *c.*1620 as a result of the wealth generated in the town from the textile and leather trades. As with many other half-timbered buildings in Ledbury, changing

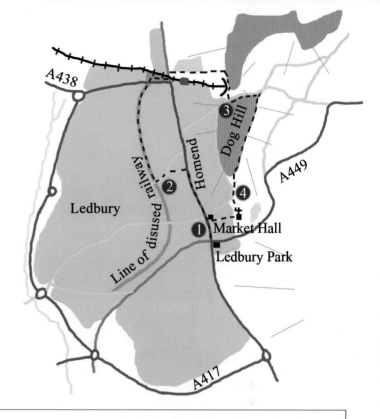

LEDBURY PARK
The half-timbered Ledbury Park was built, as the New House, in 1595 on the site of the bishop's palace, which itself had been relocated here from a few hundred yards away at the centre of the market for greater privacy and also for direct access to the bishop's hunting grounds on Malvern Chase. This second palace was abandoned in 1356 (along with those at Ross, Bromyard and elsewhere) and left to decay as the result of the Black Death which curtailed the amount of labour available.

fashions later meant that several had Georgian façades added, or were plastered over, as happened with the Feathers, until fashions turned once more.

Further on you will reach St Katherine's Almshouses on your left. The presence of the first bishop's palace, of which nothing remains, alongside the market, meant that not long after the creation of the borough, businesses spilled over into and down the Homend, giving the town its current long linear nature.

On the far side of the street you now reach, Bye Street, is the Elizabeth Barrett Browning Institute. Cross Bye Street and keep on the main street (the Homend) until you come to Belle Orchard on the left (just past the Methodist Church on the other side of the Homend).

ST KATHERINE'S ALMSHOUSES

These started their life as St Katherine's Hospital, founded *c.*1231 by Bishop Foliot, probably on the site of his original palace, for the poor and aged, to provide rest, warmth, cleanliness and an adequate diet, together with care of their souls. Bishop Foliot also endowed a chantry chapel as part of the complex where prayers could be said for his soul. Others followed his lead and by 1360 there were a total of six chantry priests. The detailed layout of the hospital is not known, but the residents would have slept in beds arranged down the two long sides of the hall, at one end of which would have been a chapel. The residents were provided with two meals a day, to be eaten in silence at trestle tables erected between the rows of beds. The hospital was run by a 'master' appointed by the Dean and Chapter, who oversaw several brethren, servants and farmhands. After the Black Death the hospital was no longer able to farm the lands with which it had been endowed, and leased them out. This generated significant profits, often misused by the master, who was apparently allowed to squander the resources at his disposal. The management of the almshouses carried on in much the same way until amended by a private Act of Parliament in 1819, after which some of the buildings were demolished. The site now largely lies under a car park, but the hall and chapel that were rebuilt *c.*1330-40 remain.

ELIZABETH BARRETT BROWNING INSTITUTE

This was built in 1895 in a Tudor revival design by Brightwen Binyon, having been chosen above 44 other potential designs, to house a reading room, library and meeting rooms. It was named after the poet Elizabeth Barrett Browning, who spent most of her youth at nearby Hope End. (For more on Hope End and Elizabeth see p.158.)

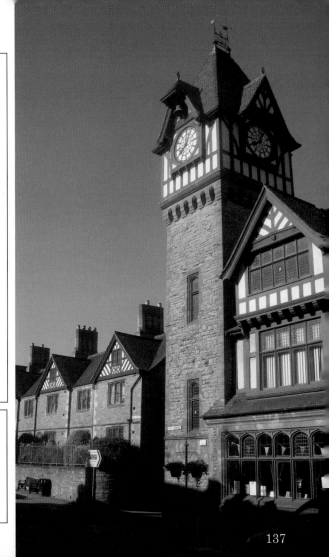

137

LEDBURY'S CANAL & RAILWAYS

The canal from Gloucester reached to within a mile of Ledbury in 1798, but work on the section to Hereford did not begin until the 1830s. (For more information see p.145.) The railway between Hereford and Worcester, on which there was a station at Ledbury amongst other places, opened in 1861, but in 1870 there were still four barge owners listed in the town. However, by 1885 the Gloucester to Ledbury railway had opened, in part constructed on the line of the canal, and it is along the line of this railway that you walk.

Turn left down this and follow it down to Orchard Lane. Turn left on this. Pass the sports field on your left and then go up the path that leads up the railway embankment to the left of the bridge. At the top, turn right to cross the bridge and follow the old railway line.

2 Walk along this for about a quarter of a mile, crossing a road after which the path leads down to near the current railway bridge. Turn left under the railway bridge, to then turn right almost immediately across a stile onto a footpath. This footpath rises uphill, following the field boundary on your right and as it reaches the woodland higher up the hillside, it bends right and passes through a gate onto a lane. Turn right on this lane and follow it along till it meets a minor road.

3 Cross the road, climb the steps and turn left on a path above the road on the far side, and then use this to follow the course of the road through the semi-ancient woodland which grows on a mix of bedrocks giving rise to a wide variety of species.

At the top of the hill you will meet a track on which you turn right. Follow the track along the hillside – this was once the route of the old coach road between Hereford and Worcester, which rose up the hillside from the site of the Market Hall. The track eventually bends to the right and downhill. Here take the path

ahead (past a grassed area with benches on your left) and follow it a short distance till it meets a road.

4 Turn left on the road (in effect keeping straight ahead) and on the bend ahead take the path off to the left into the churchyard. From the churchyard, take Church Lane back to your starting point, passing Church House (near the top of the street, on the left) built *c.*1600, the old grammar school, now a heritage centre (on the right), Ledbury Museum and Ledbury Town Council offices (both towards the bottom of the street). The museum's building used to be in Butcher's Row and was due for demolition shortly after the Napoleonic wars, but it was dismantled and re-erected first in the back garden of a house in the High Street and then in its present position in 1979 to serve as a museum run by Ledbury & District Civic Society. (For further details see www.ledburycivicsociety.org/butcher-row-house-museum; it tends to be open on set days of the week from Easter till the end of October.) The building that houses the town council offices was erected in the Tudor period and contains wall paintings of the period that can be seen at certain times.

LEDBURY CHURCH

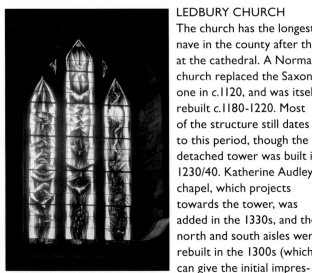

The church has the longest nave in the county after that at the cathedral. A Norman church replaced the Saxon one in c.1120, and was itself rebuilt c.1180-1220. Most of the structure still dates to this period, though the detached tower was built in 1230/40. Katherine Audley's chapel, which projects towards the tower, was added in the 1330s, and the north and south aisles were rebuilt in the 1300s (which can give the initial impression from the outside that the whole church belongs to this period). There are a number of fine monuments, including the effigy of a priest in vestments from the mid 13th century; a 14th-century effigy of a lady on a tomb chest; a large wall monument to Edward Skynner and his wife of the 1630s; and a clutch of memorials in the south aisle including ones by John Flaxman and Sir Richard Westmacott. The church also includes an array of stained glass, with fragments of medieval glass in the Audley Chapel, a series of windows by Charles Eamer Kempe, and modern glass by John K. Clark in the north aisle above the Biddulph family pew.

141

Walk 21
Ashperton
& the Ledbury Canal

5.75 miles, largely on minor roads, paths across or along field edges, tracks, and woodland paths. Only a few stiles. Includes two churches, a castle site, a stretch of canal, and hop kilns.

Park in the car park by the church at Ashperton (GR 643 415). (The church is signalled by a brown sign pointing to the west off the A417.)

1 From the car park, take the footpath through the churchyard to the right of the church and out through a gate, the path then leading past the moated site of Ashperton Castle on your right. At a corner of the moat soon reached, the path continues ahead through the woodland to reach a kissing gate into a field. Here, take the right-hand of the two waymarked public paths, and head diagonally across the field to its far corner, keeping to the left of a fishing lake. Go through the gate at the far corner of the field, then walk along the track by the trees that screen some poultry houses on your left. After 100 yards or so, where the track bends left, a footpath turns sharp right to head across the corner of the field aiming for a point some 10 yards to the left of the corner of the field you have recently crossed. Cross the stream here by the bridge, then cross the hill slope beyond on much the same line, heading just to the left of the left-hand of two groups of three large trees near the far field boundary. Near these trees you cross into the

ASHPERTON CHURCH & CASTLE

The nave, transepts and chancel of the church date mainly from the 14th century, with a tower built in 1800. The castle mound is oval and surrounded by an almost square moat, approached by a causeway on the eastern side. There are traces of a roughly rectangular earthwork to the east, where the church stands, and indications of a possible hall block. William de Grandison had a licence to crenellate the castle in 1292. William was heir of Otto Grandson, head of the English branch of a Savoyard family whose principal residence was Grandson Castle near Lake Neufchâtel and who at some point seem to have added an i to their name. Otto is a character largely forgotten to Herefordshire history. Described as 'a brave soldier and brilliant diplomat', he was a close friend and confidant of Edward I, believed by some to have been the person who sucked the poison from the wound when Edward, as prince, suffered an assassination attempt in the Holy Land. He was entrusted with diplomatic missions to Gascony and the Holy Land, was often in charge of Edward's armies in the Marches and was co-leader of the force that captured Anglesey in the Welsh wars. When William's lands were seized, at a time when there was a reaction to the perceived power of 'aliens', he gained protection from Edmund, earl of Lancaster, in whose service he was, and received letters of protection from Edward I whilst engaged in fortifying the new castle at Caernarvon. In 1304 he was governor of Jersey and Guernsey. He was summoned to Parliament from between 1299 and 1325, and was also at the coronation of Edward II. He died in 1335. What remained of William's castle was largely grubbed out when trees were planted on the site at the end of the 18th century.

next field and turn slightly right, your 'target' now being the left-hand end of a roof with two dormer windows, the rest of the house being hidden by the rise in the ground. The path passes immediately alongside the left-hand side of this house, via a gate, and so between houses and down to the A417.

2 Cross the A417 and walk between the village hall on your left and the war memorial on your right to a gate into a field. The path you want from the signposted choice offered is that which crosses the field almost diagonally towards the far corner, passing to the right of a group of trees that stand not far into the field, the footpath gate out of this field being just to the right of a sunken copse that protrudes into the field, not the field gate that is in the far corner.

Once through this gate, head diagonally across the next field towards a building to the left of an orchard. The path passes through a gate at this point, and you'll enter onto a cricket pitch, the building now becoming apparent as a cricket pavilion. Yet again there is a choice of waymarked paths here, the one you want being that which crosses the cricket pitch, just to the right of the square. Clearly if a game is in progress you should walk around the edge of the ground! As you cross, notice the humped earth on your left beyond the pitch, and the lines of trees that continue from near each end. The former lies above a canal tunnel, whilst the trees also mark the line of the sunken canal.

Once across the stile on the far side of the cricket pitch, the path stays on much the same line, crossing the field to

THE HEREFORD & GLOUCESTER CANAL

The first plans for a canal to link Hereford and Gloucester were made in 1777 as part of a grander plan that would have also seen Leominster connected to the canal system. Nothing came of that proposal, and plans for a canal linking the two cities, this time via Ledbury, resurfaced in 1790, to be partly funded by a branch to service some coal mines at Newent. The potential cost meant that many favoured a proposal to enhance the navigability of the Wye instead, but the discovery of more coal at Newent swung the financial pendulum in favour of the canal. An Act of Parliament empowering its construction was granted in April 1791. Subsequently it was decided that the canal proper would pass through Newent, with a shorter offshoot to the coal mines, and by 1795 the section from Gloucester to Newent was open. But the new route required a tunnel at Oxenhall on the Ledbury side of Newent, the construction of which was causing problems due to the amount of water entering the 20 shafts which had been constructed so that work could proceed simultaneously on several workfaces. As a result costs escalated, and construction ceased one mile short of Ledbury in 1798; the coal at Newent proved to be of low quality, and income generated was less than hoped for. There the canal remained till 1832, when it was extended a short distance to service the Ledbury gas works.

Then, in 1839, a new Act of Parliament was obtained to allow the company to raise the money required to complete the canal. Work started in November of that year and the canal was opened in stages as they were completed, finally reaching the Hereford basin on 22 May 1845. On this section of the canal it was the Ashperton tunnel that caused the problems. Although only 400 yards long, water flooded the work surfaces as with the Oxenhall tunnel, whilst the rock proved unstable, requiring a brick and stone lining. To oversee the work, Stephen Ballard, the engineer responsible for the canal's construction, built a house nearby from the bricks being used to line the tunnel, essentially simply piling the bricks on top of each other and with little use of mortar, so that he could live on site. Largely as a result of the additional work required on the Ashperton tunnel, the section from Ledbury to Hereford cost almost three times what had been estimated. Efforts to boost traffic on the canal were so successful that a timetable for the transit of the Oxenhall tunnel had to be introduced in 1849. This didn't always work. In May 1851 the *Hereford Times* carried a story about an incident in which boats travelling in opposite directions had met in the middle, neither giving way for two and a half days. But the canal proved to be the cause of its own downfall, for some of its income derived from boats carrying materials for the construction of railways, and in 1862 the canal was leased to the Great Western and West Midland Railway, who wished to convert parts of the route into a railway line. In 1881, half of the canal was duly closed and sections were used for the line of the Ledbury and Gloucester Railway. The Hereford to Ledbury section remained open, but gradually became disused. The canal company was only formally wound up when the railways were nationalised in 1948.

its far right-hand corner where you cross a stile out onto a minor road on your right.

3 Turn left on the road. Almost immediately you'll come to a building marked with the sign 'Tunnel House'. Along this stretch of road, glimpses can be had of the canal from time to time, it obviously being more clear of vegetation in winter. Continue along the road, which in due course turns to cross the canal and head away from it, before gradually closing back in on the line of the canal.

4 Close to the canal, take the road to the right (in fact the first road junction you will come to) and recross the canal. You are very much in old hop country here; many of the farms you will pass on the rest of the walk still have

HOP KILNS

Herefordshire still grows hops – not to the extent that it once did, but there are plentiful reminders of the industry, now considerably mechanised and centralised, in the buildings that were once hop kilns. Some of these have been converted to houses, others remain as components of farm buildings, often with their 'witch's hat' cowl still rotating in the wind. The English used to drink ale which contained no hops and so was much sweeter and darker than present English real ales, more akin to a stout. The bitter taste of hops initially found an unwilling public, but as their preservative value came to be appreciated and taste-buds started to adjust, imports began, largely from Holland. As demand increased, this led to hops being grown in Kent from 1524. Parts of Herefordshire were also found suitable, with their combination of clay soil that can retain the water needed by the plants and alluvial soil that aids drainage. High hedges were grown round the hopyards to protect the plants from the wind. By the late 1800s and early 1900s the autumn saw special trains laid on to bring hop pickers from Birmingham and the Black Country. Whole families would come, treating it as both an annual holiday and a chance to earn some extra money, often staying in the farmer's barns. Once picked, the hops would be laid on a horsehair or equivalent cloth over slats above a furnace in the kiln to dry. These kilns were originally built 16 foot square, but later it was felt that round kilns would give a more even heat and became the order of the day, built with a diameter of 16 feet. These were more expensive to build and were found in practice to be little better at drying the hops, so square kilns took over once again. The revolving cowl at the top encouraged a through draft and prevented a downward one. With the U-Boat threat in the First World War, some land was taken out of hop production to grow more food, then increasing productivity in the early 1920s meant there was a surplus, and some farmers decided to stop growing hops when it was time to renew the wirework or the hop plants (then required about every 20-25 years). In more recent years, dwarf hop plants have become more common, some farmers judging that they are easier to grow and pick by machine. Herefordshire is still one of the main hop-growing counties, along with Worcestershire and Kent.

the 'witch's' hat' cowls above what were the hop kilns. Pass Swinmore Farm, then the road bends to the right and in due course comes to another road junction.

5 Turn right here (in effect carrying on straight ahead) and this brings you past Munsley Court with the remains of its hop kilns, soon after which you turn right on a lane signposted to Munsley Church, which you may wish to visit when you reach it on your right. Where the track to the right leads to the church, the circular walk bears left on the track just before the gate to Lower Court and half circles a moated site, to later pass by a lake on your left and then cross a stream. Shortly after crossing the stream, the track enters a field and then keeps to the hedgerow on your right-hand side to leave the field at its far end onto a track near Nupend Farm. Keep on this track, which gains a tarmacked surface and bears slightly right at the entrance to the farm.

6 At the next, recently refurbished, group of farm buildings (White House Farm and Oakville) which you reach on your right at a bend in the road, take the footpath slightly to the right of the line you've just been walking; the path passes to the immediate left of the group of buildings and heads into the orchards beyond. Once in the orchards, initially keep to the boundary on your left, and cross a stile into another orchard beyond. Again, keep to the boundary on your left, but when this curves away slightly the path technically keeps straight

LOWER COURT AND MUNSLEY CHURCH
Norman elements remain in some herringbone masonry in the east wall of the church, in the chancel arch and in two small round-headed windows, but the rest of the church is largely Victorian.

The mound on which Lower Court sits was probably originally a castle mound surrounded by a partial moat and marshy area probably filled from the stream to the east. Some of the moat has subsequently been filled in. The bailey was to the south-east of the mound. At the time of the Domesday Survey Munsley was held by William fitz Baderon, who was perhaps responsible for any early castle.

ahead through the orchard, though you may prefer to keep to the field boundary. At the far end of the orchard, the path leaves it through a gap in the hedge next to a large oak.

7 Cross the lane and walk up the path ahead, which passes along the edge of gardens to enter a field. Follow the hedgeline on your right, and cross the stile on your right at the far end of the field. Turn left and immediately left again to follow the hedge on your left to a kissing gate. Through this, follow the path alongside the house on your right down to the A417. Cross this and take the road back down to the church.

Walk 23
Coddington
& Colwall Church

5.25 miles, largely on paths and minor roads. Many stiles. Includes two churches, a church ale house and the valley where Elizabeth Barrett Browning once lived.

CODDINGTON CHURCH
Essentially a 13th-century church with a fine medieval roof, with a tower added in 1865 to the design of F.R. Kempson. The east window was made by Morris & Co. (the design is by Edward Burne-Jones) and the altar frontals are also by Morris & Co. There is a medieval cross base and shaft in the churchyard.

Park in the car park next to the church at Coddington (GR 718 427).

① Turn right out of the car park and walk down the lane, keeping right at the road junction by the churchyard. Walk on past Church Farm; ignore the next lane on your right (signposted to Woofields), but at the next junction, turn right on the road signposted to Wellington Heath. Follow the road until you reach a turning to the left in front of a house (there's a letterbox on the corner). Turn left here, and just beyond the entrance to Pithouse Farm on the left, cross a stile on the right, just to the right of a gateway. Go straight ahead across the field to another stile; cross it and follow the fenceline on your left to reach and cross another stile, a track and then a further stile. Keep following the same line along the

COLWALL CHURCH & ALE HOUSE

The church now stands separate from the village, the centre of which shifted to cluster around the railway station. A late Norman doorway opens into an Early English south aisle, itself separated from the nave by a 13th-century arcade with carvings of foliage and human heads on some of the capitals. The nave has a fine medieval roof with pairs of collar-beams and windbraces. The chancel dates from 1865, the north aisle from 1880. There is a Jacobean pulpit. On the north wall is a 13th-century tile, originally one of twelve, referring to the months of the working year. The remaining tile represents March and shows a man digging.

The ale house was built with long diagonal braces in the early 1530s, a date discovered as a result of dendrochronology (which also discovered that the timber was felled from a number of woodlands). Although this is a rare survivor of such an establishment, church ale houses were once relatively common, and were used to brew and sell ale to raise funds for the church. But the increasing Puritanism of the early 1600s was to do for them. In this instance the bishop of Hereford felt that sales of ale had reached too high a level, and the building was sold in 1614 to become an almshouse. It was last occupied in the 1930s and then fell into disrepair. The building was repaired during the 1980s to become the church hall.

edge of the next field, cross another stile, and keep going across the next field. Then cross another stile and you will find yourself in an orchard.

Keep going in the same direction, along the left-hand edge of the orchard, and just before you reach the far end of the orchard, turn left and cross a stream via a footbridge with a stile at each end. At the far side of the bridge, turn right and follow the field boundary on your right. At the end of the field, cross a stile to emerge on a lane.

❷ Turn left along the lane; then, after 50 yards or so, cross a stile on the right. Cross the field, aiming for the left-hand of the dips in the ridge of the Malvern Hills on the horizon. (Depending on the stage of crop growth, it may be easier to follow the verges round the edge of the field.) In the middle of the field boundary on the far side there's a stile; cross this and walk along a short stretch of path that leads to a bridge over the stream. Cross the bridge and walk across the next field (the path is slightly to the left of a line of telegraph

poles). On the other side of the field go through a field gate and cross a short stretch of ground to meet a track on which you turn right. Walk along the track (you may need to go round a gate you almost immediately meet by a slightly hidden style to its left), keeping straight ahead. You may be able to get a good view of British Camp on its hilltop over to your left. When you reach a road junction near Colwall church, cross the road and go straight ahead to then turn right past the timber-framed church alehouse to enter the churchyard.

3 Walk through the churchyard and on the other side, take the road ahead. When you come to a T-junction, turn right. After 20 yards or so, cross a stile on the left into an orchard. (Use the field gate if the stile is overgrown.) Follow the field boundary on the left uphill (again there are views of British Camp over your left shoulder as you climb). Cross the stile at the top left-hand corner of the orchard and walk up the path into the woodland. Over another stile, keep straight ahead along the left-hand edge of a sloping meadow. Then cross another stile and

go up the steps through the woods; then another stile will take you into a field where you continue up the hillside, keeping the edge of the woodland on your left. Cross another stile in the corner of the field and follow the metal fence on your left. Cross a stile at the top left of the meadow, after which the path bears right across the next field to join a track which runs along the bottom of the grassy bank ahead of you.

Turn right on this track, and after a while, just before a field gate crosses it, turn left up a path that heads steeply uphill. Follow the path to the trig point at the top of Oyster Hill ('oyster' meant 'sheepfold' in Old English), from which there's a wonderful view to the west, from the Black Mountains all the way round to the Clee Hills.

4 The path leads past the trig point (and a friendly bench) along the ridge; then go through a wooden field gate and follow the path between meadows on your left and woodland on your right. In due course Hope End House will come into view on your left (rather obscured

HOPE END & ELIZABETH BARRETT BROWNING

Edward Moulton Barrett bought the 475-acre estate in 1809 and moved there with his three daughters, of whom Elizabeth was the eldest. He had made his money in the West Indies sugar business, and set about building a new house, converting the old one to a stable. He chose John Claudius Loudon to carry out the work to both house and gardens. For the house Loudon chose what was called the 'hindoo' style, in reality more Islamic with ogee curves to windows and the addition of minarets; and he opted for a 'gardenesque' style (a term of his own coinage) for the garden plantings, some of which remain. Elizabeth started to compose poetry at a young age, and at only 11 and 12 wrote the epic *Battle of Marathon* in four volumes. She suffered a riding accident when aged 15 and was an invalid thereafter. In 1828 her mother died, then her father had to sell the estate in 1831 to satisfy the gathering creditors after his business failed. The family moved first to Sidmouth, then to London, where Elizabeth eloped with Robert Browning. In 1873 new owners demolished the house that Edward built, building their own Hope End nearby.

by trees in summer). Go through a metal footpath gate and keep following the path, which swings left and then right through a meadow. (From here there's a good view of what was Hope End House's walled garden.) At the far left-hand corner of the meadow, go through a footpath gate onto a lane next to Upper Lodge.

5 Turn right along the lane. You'll immediately come to a T-junction with a minor road; turn right along this. You'll shortly come to a footpath on the right which leads to Loxter Ashbed Quarry. (This is a private site, but group visits can be organised; if you'd be interested to see this disused limestone quarry, whose geology dates from the Silurian period, phone Mandy on 01531 634303.) Keep going along the road, and at the next road junction, turn right up Raycombe Lane. The lane follows the edge of woodland; at a point where there's a break in the trees and just past Raycombe House, where there's a timber-framed house up on the bank to your right, take the footpath on the left through a footpath gate and then over a stile. The path bears down and across a very large field, heading for Coddington church spire, which you'll see in the distance, and a corner of hedgerow that juts out into the field. Pass just to the left of this corner and the house behind it, and leave the field by a stile/field gate in the corner of the field beyond. In the next field follow the hedgerow on your left, and go through a gateway at its end into the next field. Walk straight across this field, keeping just to the right of the two-pole electricity pylon and aiming for the field gate with a stile to its right in the far fenceline. Cross this stile and in this next field head towards a field gate adjacent to the corner of the land around the farmhouse. When you reach the gate, turn right in front of it, and follow the field boundary on your left to the far corner of the field, where you will find a stile. Cross this and turn right to walk to the end of the field, which you leave by another stile and emerge onto a lane.

6 Cross the lane and turn right; in about 10 yards, go through a narrow gap in the tall hedge on your left and cross a bridge; then follow the path between a tree and an ornamental pond, and up between the rows of vines of Coddington Vineyard. (The path is between the ninth and tenth rows from the right.) At the top of the vineyard, turn left and leave it through a wooden kissing gate. Walk along a short stretch of path and then cross two stiles on the right in quick succession. Turn left and follow the hedged (on one side) and fenced (on the other) path to a stile. Cross this and turn right on a track, and when you come to a lane, turn left to return to Coddington church.

Walk 24
British Camp
& Little Malvern Priory

3.5 miles, largely on grassy tracks and woodland paths, with some main road (with pavements). No stiles. Includes a major hillfort and associated Norman castle motte, the Shire Ditch, and Little Malvern Priory. Purists will recognize that the priory is in Worcestershire, but as Herefordshire likes to claim William Langland and the Vision of Piers the Plowman *which has connections with the priory as its own, it is included here. You may want to check the opening times for the gardens next to Little Malvern Priory (see p.165).*

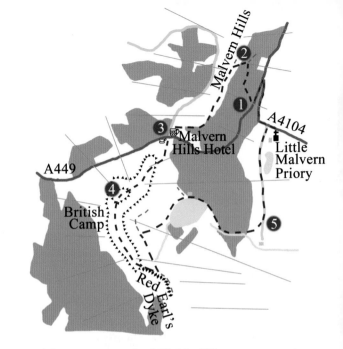

For the start of this walk, we have chosen a layby on the A449 just beyond the crest of the ridge where the main British Camp car park is located, on the Worcestershire side of the hills (GR 768 406). This means less of an uphill climb towards the end of your walk.

1 From this lay-by, take the narrow footpath from near its centre (the right-hand one of the two paths that leave the layby) which slants up and across the hills heading north (towards Great Malvern). This path will meet another about half-way up the hillside, on which you turn right to contour the hillside. When you come to a crossroads of paths and tracks, turn sharp left to continue up the hillside and you will emerge on the crest of the ridge between two of its summits.

2 Turn left, and take the left of two paths to walk over and down one summit, catching good views of British Camp ahead of you. Pass two houses on your right, then the path swings to the right and slightly uphill, then drops down to a minor road near the Malvern Hills Hotel.

BRITISH CAMP

The original defences, formed from material taken from both the ditches and an internal scoop quarry, covered an area of about 8 acres with entrances to the south and north-east, an area later extended to the north and south to enclose a total of some 32 acres. The extended hillfort had four entrances. Excavations have revealed that the site was covered with rectangular four-post buildings that may have been grain stores or houses, built on small terraces that are still visible in a low sun. If lived in permanently, a problem would have been a water supply. A partial solution might have been to collect rainwater off the thatched roofs of the buildings, but it would also have been necessary to collect water from streams down the hillside. This would probably have been considered quite normal, for early societies across the world have often had to travel far to collect a supply of wholesome water; in many parts of rural Africa this is still the norm. A lack of a permanent water supply would, of course, have made such hillforts vulnerable to the siege tactics employed by the Romans, as opposed to the more hit and run tactics used by Celtic peoples. (See also the box on Midsummer Hill on p.171.)

MYSTERY CASTLE

On the hilltop at the centre of British Camp a further earthwork has been created consisting of an oval mound surrounded by a ditch (known as 'the Citadel'), whilst a further ditch to the north-west cuts across the Iron Age hillfort, the whole creating what appears to be a Norman motte and bailey castle. Excavations in the 1950s revealed some 12th-century pottery, which gives strength to this theory, and stone found on the site indicates that the motte could have been capped by a shell keep. It has also been suggested that the mounds flanking the ridgeway approach from the south represent the remains of a gateway. But who built a castle and when remains a mystery. Whilst the building of a castle in Norman times high on a hill and distant from any settlement was rare, it did sometimes happen. There are three main possibilities. First, it may have been built soon after the Norman Conquest, though there is no written record of its construction. Secondly, perhaps it was constructed as a hunting lodge during the disputes between Earl Gilbert de Clare and the bishop of Hereford (see under Shire Ditch, p.173); or thirdly, it may have been built when the supporters of Matilda were fighting King Stephen, with opposing armies contesting control of the cities of Worcester and Hereford – though the work required would have been a major undertaking in the face of the shifting fortunes of a very fluid war.

③ Turn left on the road, cross the main road to the British Camp car park, and take the path that leads out of the car park at the corner where it adjoins the main road. The zig-zag tarmac/stony path/steps that you soon reach on your right will take you all the way to the summit of British Camp.

④ From the summit, continue into the southern arm of the camp. You may wish to continue along the ridge for a while (and even join up with walk no.25), but for this circular route, walk to the far end of the camp and descend the steps that curl down the hillside near the Shire Ditch (see p.173), which runs along the hillside to your left, then turn left down the gravelled path towards the reservoir. Before long, turn right on a path that leads down the hillside to the track along the left-hand side of the reservoir and past a house, to join a concrete track which leads downhill. Not long after this track loses its concrete surface it continues with a stream on its right. Just before the stream crosses the path you're on, turn left onto a smaller path,

keeping the stream on your right, and continuing through the woodland to enter a field by a gate. The path crosses the field, staying just to the left of a lime tree standing immediately inside the field and aiming for a gate just to the right of the yew on the far side of the field.

5 Through this gate, turn left and follow the lane along to the main road, passing the topiary of The Court. At the road, turn right and take the last of the series of gates on the right to visit the priory. Return up the road along the pavement and continue on this as it bends right. At the junction with the A449, turn left and follow the pavement to the layby where you parked.

LITTLE MALVERN PRIORY

The priory was founded as a daughter house of Worcester Cathedral in 1125 and, as its name suggests, was always small with around 12 monks, with the number having dropped to five at the time of its dissolution in 1534. Today's building is what was the chancel and crossing tower of the priory church. On the basis that when it was extensively rebuilt by Bishop Alcock between 1480 and 1482, the old chancel included much Perpendicular work (including its east window), it is probable that the tower was once capped with Perpendicular-style battlements and pinnacles, though it now carries a pyramidal roof. Alcock was so appalled at the lax state of affairs at the priory when he visited in 1480 that he sent the monks away to Gloucester Priory for correction whilst the rebuilding proceeded. The building has several now blocked doorways and openings that once led off to other parts of the complex: those behind the altar led to a Lady Chapel or vestries; those to the side gave access to or looked into side chapels. The wooden stalls, once set beneath the tower, contain the damaged remains of misericords, though the carvings on the handrests survive. The stained glass in the east window dates to the rebuilding and has rare images of the Yorkist royal family of Edward IV, though not of the king himself.

At the Dissolution the buildings and adjoining land passed to Henry Russell, in whose family and those of his descendants, the Berringtons, they have remained ever since. Little Malvern Court contains the core of the 14th-century refectory, and the grounds include the remains of the fishponds. The outline of the original nave is also marked out.

The priory is open every day during daylight hours. Little Malvern Court gardens tend to be open on some days from mid April to mid July, but for up-to-date details check www.littlemalverncourt.co.uk.

WILLIAM LANGLAND AND PIERS PLOWMAN

William Langland is believed to have been educated at Little Malvern Priory. He may have been a son of the de Rokayles, tenants of the Despensers, possibly born illegitimate. In 1335 or 1336 he moved to Cornhill in London with his wife Kit and daughter Calote, where he earned a living from clerical work. His poem, *Piers Plowman,* exists in three texts, two of them a worked-over and amended version of the previous one. The earliest was written in the late 1360s, the second in the late 1370s whilst he still lived in London, and the third in the 1380s or '90s after Langland had returned to Malvern, and where he died around 1398.

The writing is a series of visions, sometimes one within another, concerned with a search, initially for money and then for truth – which is deemed to be more important. The dreamer is called Long Will, the titular hero, Piers the Plowman cropping up as a character in the story who offers himself as a guide. In his search, Long Will meets a range of folk from the society of the day, rather as Chaucer does in his *Canterbury Tales.* In Will's case they include ploughmen, merchants, minstrels, friars, jugglers, a knight and members of the clergy. As his thoughts develop he feels that everything in the world possesses order except for its one rational being – man. For this, the clergy start to bear the brunt of his ire, though not exclusively. He begins to feel that the solution is love, which the clergy should preach and practise together with acts of charity. From the clergy's love of man will come the true love of God. As the poem concludes by accepting the structure of society as it is, it is certainly not revolutionary in intent, but it does consider ethical questions of wealth, inheritance and hierarchy and suggest models of community ownership and moderate provision for all, with the Commons exercising some power over the Crown. It is these suggestions, together with the fact that a ploughman was the central character, that led to Piers Plowman being one of the rallying cries during the Peasants' Revolt in 1381.

The poem begins on the Malvern Hills, where Long Will falls asleep and has a vision of a tower set upon a hill and a fortress in a deep valley; between these symbols of heaven and hell is a 'fair field full of folk', representing the world of mankind.

Walk 25
Midsummer Hill
& Obelisk

3 miles, largely on tracks and woodland paths. No stiles. Includes a hillfort, a commemorative obelisk with wide views across Bronsil Castle to Eastnor, and the Shire Ditch.

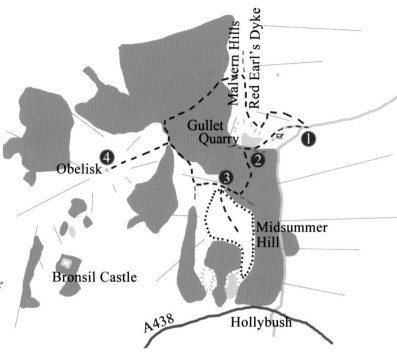

This walk is partly in Worcestershire! It starts from a Malvern Hills Conservators car park (Swinyard Car Park, cost £4.60 at time of writing) on Castlemorton Common (GR 765 382), most easily reached by taking the A438 from near Ledbury towards Tewkesbury. Having crossed the ridge of the Malvern Hills in the village of Hollybush, take the road to the left at the first crossroads. Follow this road along through woodland till it emerges onto the common, the car park then being immediately on your right.

① Turn left out of the car park. The lane you're on turns left, but you go straight on, on a tarmacked lane off the road that serves the car park and leads into a cleft in the hills. You may wish to note a café on the left here for your return, its opening hours depending upon the time of year. Continue along the lane to its end at Gullet Quarry, with its impressive cliffs and lagoon. Follow the path along the left-hand side of the lagoon to a junction of paths at its far end.

② Turn right along a wide path, and about 40 yards later, turn left along a smaller one that wends its way up through trees and between shoulders of hill to eventually

MIDSUMMER HILL

This hillfort was subjected to much amateur archaeological excavation in the 1800s and early 1900s, which confused the picture. More recent work, notably a series of excavations between 1965 and 1970 by Dr Stanley Stanford, showed that the double rampart, which encloses an area of some 21 acres, was built around 390BC, though finds of Bronze Age pottery indicate earlier use of the site, perhaps for burials. Given the gravelly and thin nature of the soil, the builders decided to strengthen the ramparts with a stone facing, selecting an outcrop of sandstone about a mile away which split into easily jointed and more regularly shaped building material than the igneous rock below the hillfort. In the rampart were two entrances formed by an inturning of the banks, a common feature in the early years of hillfort construction before gateways became more elaborate. Small terraces were found on which rectangular structures were built and replaced over the years, usually around posts dug into the ground, but sometimes erected from a cill beam laid on the ground – the form of construction used in medieval 'black and white' box-framed cottages. The roofs were probably covered in thatch or hide as no evidence of tiles was found. Other hut sites are represented by grooves or scoops in the ground, the huts being built in areas where the topsoil had been scraped off to help form the ramparts. It is estimated that the population associated with the hillfort may have numbered between 1,300 and 1,500 people. Unlike most hillforts, Midsummer Hill's ramparts enclosed a small pool near the southern gate, where water was collected in stone-lined sumps. No evidence was found for querns for grinding grain, but some was found for ovens for baking bread. Many of the structures contained evidence of fire pits, suggesting at least semi-permanent occupation. Detailed excavations at the southern gateway produced evidence for 17 successive pairs of gateposts, spanning a period of around 450 years, the end coinciding with the arrival of the Romans in 48AD. It also seems that many of the huts were burnt to the ground at around this date, perhaps a sign of attack, or at least abandonment, although finds of nails and some pot sherds indicate at least some use of the site during the Roman or Romano-British period. Assuming the evidence is correctly interpreted to indicate that the site was permanently occupied over a number of years, one wonders why such a windy site was chosen, and what the relationship was with the settlement of the British Camp, just along the ridge.

reach the ridge of the shoulder on your left. At a crossroads of paths, turn right and the path will lead you out onto the other shoulder, just below the ramparts of Midsummer Hill hillfort, where it joins a further path.

3 Initially, turn left on this path and walk to the crest of Midsummer Hill, with its expansive views. To the west you can see Eastnor Castle. Buried in woodland in the valley immediately below you and almost in a direct line to Eastnor are the remains of Bronsil Castle. To the right of these is the obelisk that will be visited later in the walk.

Return down the path to the ramparts where you

OBELISK

The obelisk was erected by John, Lord Somers, at the time that Eastnor Castle was being constructed, to commemorate his father, who had been Lord High Chancellor of England, his eldest son, who was killed at the Battle of Burgos in the Peninsular War, and also an earlier relative, Ensign James Cocks, who was killed fighting the French in 1758 during the Seven Years War.

entered Midsummer Hill hillfort, and stay on this path as it swings left. It will meet a lane on which you turn right and walk up to a junction of paths and tracks. Here, go through the gate next to the cattle grid on your left, and then go straight ahead on the track to the obelisk.

4 From the obelisk, return to the cattle grid, pass through the gate alongside it, and then turn left on the track. Keep following this through the woodland. When you reach another cattle grid and gate across the track, take the footpath gate to their right up on a bank, and follow the path beyond that leads up the hill to the ridge of the Malverns and the line of the Shire Ditch. From here you can turn left and walk along to join up with Walk 24, or turn right and follow the ridge. There is a choice of routes down to the car park. One leads directly down the hillside, but if you keep going to a point above the cliff face at the top of Gullet Quarry, you can find a path that takes a more gentle curve down the hillside.

THE SHIRE DITCH

It is generally accepted that the Shire Ditch was built *c.*1287 by Gilbert de Clare, earl of Gloucester, as a boundary between his estates and those of the bishop of Hereford after arguments had broken out over the hunting of deer. De Clare had been gradually encroaching on the estates of the bishop on the western flank of the hills. Eventually accepting that he was in the wrong, he constructed the ditch to prevent deer he was hunting from escaping onto the bishop's lands. The nature of the 'ditch' varies throughout its course along the ridge of the Malverns, being in places now a bank some three feet high with a ditch one foot deep on its western side, in others a bank with a ditch on both sides, and sometimes the western ditch can measure 18 feet wide. As the ditch is mentioned in two Anglo-Saxon charters, it must predate the dispute between de Clare and the bishop, albeit still being a boundary marker. Archaeological work has now shown that the bank was built in two stages, one after the construction of the hill-forts (and so possibly relating to de Clare's work), but one before. It probably represents a very ancient territorial divide.

EASTNOR CASTLE

Eastnor Castle was designed by Robert Smirke for the first Lord Somers in 1815. It is rectangular in plan and Norman revivalist in style, with crenellated parapets and round towers at each corner. In 1849 A.W.N. Pugin was employed to redesign part of the interior, including the decoration of the Gothic Drawing Room. Today the castle is open to the public on certain days of the year between Easter and September; see www.eastnorcastle.com.

BRONSIL CASTLE

In this photograph, the site of Bronsil Castle can be seen in the bottom of the valley behind a line of lighter colour trees; the large building above and to the right of the site is Eastnor Castle. Sir John Beauchamp, Lord Treasurer of England, was created Lord Beauchamp by Henry VI, and it was his son Richard, the second Lord Beauchamp, who obtained a licence from King Henry in 1449 to crenellate the family mansion at Bronsil and empark 300 acres of land. The third Lord Beauchamp died without issue and the ownership passed via the Talbot earls of Shrewsbury to the Reed family. It seems that they had abandoned it by the early 17th century and it might have been damaged by fire either during or some time shortly after the Civil War. It was certainly ruinous by 1731. Curtain walls with towers at the corners and the midpoints enclosed an island some 40 yards square that sat within a wet moat, itself surrounded by a second dry moat. The island and moats are still there, but the walls have largely tumbled away and the island has become covered in thick vegetation.

Walk 26
Much Marcle

5 miles, largely on paths across fields or alongside field boundaries, minor roads and the Herefordshire Trail. Several stiles. Includes a church, Westons Cider and a possible excursion to Hellens (for opening hours go to https://hellensmanor.com).

Park near the church in Much Marcle (GR 657 327).

1 The walk begins by going into the churchyard and following the path that leads round the south of the church, passing between the 1,500-year-old yew and the entrance porch, to leave the churchyard via a gate. Cross the tarmacked lane that leads to Homme House (hidden by trees), and go over the stile into the field.

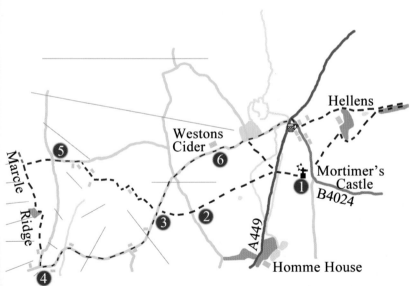

MUCH MARCLE CHURCH

The large building dates mainly from the 13th century, with north and south aisles, a central tower and north chapel off the chancel, and is notable for its tombs and effigies. The effigy in painted wood (restored in 1972) is of Walter de Helyon, who died sometime after 1357 and probably lived at nearby Hellens. It is believed that his body was buried at Ashperton, and that the effigy was brought here when the chancel of that church collapsed. He is depicted in civilian dress of the mid 14th century. There is also an elaborate tomb to Blanche Mortimer (daughter of the Roger Mortimer who ruled England in all but name in the late 1320s in consort with Edward II's wife, Isabella), wife of Sir Peter Grandison, who died in 1347; and one in black and white marble of the mid 17th century of Sir John Kyrle and his wife, Sybil Scudamore. A further chest tomb is believed to be that of Hugh Audley and his wife Isolda, who lived at Hellens in the early 1300s. In the churchyard grows a yew with a girth of over 30 feet. It is at least 1,500 years old and reputed to be one of the oldest yews in England. Inside its split trunk is a seat for up to seven people.

BARONETVS, HVIVS HEREFORDIA, COMITATVS ITERVM VICECOMES

The path heads across to almost the far right-hand corner of the field, which you leave by a pair of metal gates and footpath bridge to reach the A449. Cross this (take care) and go over a little wooden bridge into a large field. There are two paths that meet at this point; you want the one that bears slightly left across the field, aiming for a slight gap in the tree line on the far side (and passing just to the left of the third telegraph pole from the right in the line of poles that cross the field). Cross the bridge in this gap and walk across the next field in the same direction as the last and go through the gap in the hedgerow on the far side. Here you again continue on the same line, but now keeping to the right of a field boundary hedgerow. At the far end of this field you pass out onto a lane.

2 Cross the lane and take the stile that's slightly to your left to enter another field. The line of the path now turns slightly to the right, aiming for a point roughly midway along a line drawn between the lone tree that stands in the field and the TV mast on the ridge. As you crest the rise in the field, you will see that the point for which you are aiming is in fact the far right-hand corner of the field, which you leave to find yourself on a minor road.

3 Turn left on the road. You'll be following this for a mile; ignore a minor road on the left and keep following the lane you're on to cross a small brook just beyond a house on the right (Little Acre). In due course you'll reach a narrow road on the right, just this side of a house.

MORTIMER'S CASTLE

Some 50 yards north-east of the church is the motte and bailey known as Mortimer's Castle. It is first mentioned in the historical record in 1153, and it is known to have once been an early stone castle, with a shell keep, of some strength. It was granted to Edmund Mortimer (father of the Roger Mortimer who imprisoned Edward II and lived with his queen) by Edward I. Thomas Walwyn, who had been granted the castle by the last earl of March in the early 1400s, gave stone from the castle to build the church tower and only foundations of the castle now remain. The motte is clearly visible, but the semi-circular bailey to its east is now occupied by houses and gardens. Further enclosures marked by earthworks lie to the north-east.

HOMME HOUSE

The estate belonged to the Mortimers (hence the name of the castle and the tomb of Blanche Mortimer in the church) and became Crown property when Edward earl of March, heir of the Mortimers, became king as Edward IV (see pp.44-5). In 1574 the estate was bought by the Kyrle family (hence the Kyrle tomb in the church) and has remained in the possession of that family's descendants ever since. The house was rebuilt in the early 17th century, substantially altered in the middle of the 19th century and renovated at the beginning of the 21st. The parkland is said to have been landscaped by Capability Brown.

4 Turn right on this narrow road, which soon reaches another house, this time on the left. Turn into its drive to find a stile into the field above the house. Cross this stile, then follow the field boundary on your left. Here there are wide views to the west across parts of the Woolhope Dome and the Wye valley to the hills around Much Dewchurch and Aconbury.

Keep to the hedgerow on your left and in due course, in a corner of the field, you will reach another stile on your left (under an ash tree). Cross this and turn right, continuing to follow the field boundary that runs along the edge of the ridge. At the end of this field, leave it by a kissing gate and turn right on a track. Follow this down to where it makes a crossroads with minor roads.

5 Go straight over. From this point, the walk goes to Westons Cider, and to get there, you can follow either of two routes. You can continue following the road down, ignoring one turning to the left and then turning left at a crossroads. Alternatively, you can walk down the road and immediately you've passed a clutch of houses, the last of which (Upper Nuttall) has a 'Victorian' street lamp on the roadside, turn right onto a track. Follow this along till you reach the gates to Little Puckmore, where a footpath on the left leads you a few yards into a field. Once in this field follow the hedgerow on your left to the first corner, where you turn right and follow the hedgerow to the next corner. Here, cross a stile into the field that's been on your left. Now walk down the field boundary on your right and after about 80 yards you will come to a stile on your

right, which you cross to find yourself on a lane that leads to the house near whose gates you are standing. Walk down this lane to the road ahead, where you turn left. Walk down the lane to a crossroads. Go straight over and you'll reach Westons Cider after about a quarter of a mile.

6 From Westons you have two options. You can continue the walk back to Much Marcle church and your vehicle, or you can walk a bit further and get a glimpse of Hellens and also visit it if you've arranged your walk to coincide with the house's opening times.

For the first option, from Westons, carry on walking down the road, and when you reach a junction with a road off to the left, cross into the field on your right by a bridge just to the left of the field gates. Head across this field to a gap in the far hedgerow located just to the right of a telegraph pole on the far side of the field. Once through this hedgerow, keep going across the next field in much the same direction to a little wooden bridge you should recognize. Retrace your steps to the church.

For the second option, carry on down the road from Westons till you reach the A449. Cross this and head along the B4024, with the Walwyn Arms on your right. Immediately past the first house on the left, take the tarmacked drive on the left which leads to another house. Keep straight ahead past a house on the left, the drive gaining a gravelled surface and reaching a footpath gate

WESTONS CIDER

Henry Weston moved to The Bounds, the home farm of what is now Westons Cider, in 1878 as a tenant farmer of its 100 acres. Finding he could not produce enough income to support his family, he went into cider production, encouraged by Charles Radcliffe Cooke of Hellens. Henry initially supplied the cider, known as Weston's Rough, in barrels through merchants, but soon thought he could improve his products and sell direct to the public. Pressing individual varieties of apples and making blends, he sold them under the label 'Wine of the West'. Horse-powered stone mills were replaced with steam-driven mills as demand increased. Henry died in 1917, but investment continued in machinery and land, with The Bounds and neighbouring farms being acquired to increase apple production and control over the produce. The site is now a visitor attraction in its own right, with a shop, restaurant and tea room, shire horses and a play park (see www.westons-cider.co.uk for up to date details).

out into a field at its far end. Keep ahead, shadowing the field boundary on your right to pass through a gate into another field and then meet a track. Turn right on the track, but this soon bears right to pass through a gateway into the grounds of Hellens where you keep straight ahead to follow the edge of the woodland on your right. When this curves to the right, keep ahead to a kissing gate and enter the next field. Cross this to the far right-hand corner and go through another kissing gate.

At this point the definitive footpath follows the field boundary on your right towards the end of the field where you cross over the boundary and turn right to walk back down alongside the field. However, a crossing has been made where you enter the field and we suggest you take this. To do so, once through the kissing gate, turn right and head up the bank onto a path in the woodland, on which you turn right.

At the end of the wood you enter a field, which the path technically crosses diagonally to the far corner, but we suggest you follow a route marked out on the ground. Thus, follow the field boundary on your right round the edge of a pond before heading towards the far corner. (Note the modern stone circle on your left.) Here turn right on a track and walk along the edge of a thin strip of woodland to the entrance drive to Hellens. To return to Much Marcle church, turn left down the drive and cross the B4024.

HELLENS

In 1096 the manor was granted to the de Balun family, who witnessed the signing of Magna Carta by King John. It subsequently passed through the Mortimer family to Lord Audley, who was created earl of Gloucester in 1337, after the previous line of de Clare earls of Gloucester had died without male issue. The manor was leased to the Walter de Helyon whose effigy lies in the church and whose family gave their name in time to the house. In the 19th century the house was owned by Charles Radcliffe Cooke, who became the local MP and was known as the 'Member for Cider' on account of his arguing for the drink's health-giving properties. He also wrote a book called *Cider and Perry*, published in 1889. Hellens' own website says, 'Among Hellens' attractions are the haunted rooms prepared for Bloody Mary Tudor and her tutor Fetherstone; the Stone Hall and its great fireplace bearing the Black Prince's crest and the Minstrel Gallery. The Music Room has a fine frieze and panelling. The gardens are being redeveloped along Tudor and Jacobean lines, reflecting the house's history. They incorporate a rare octagonal dovecote, a walled knot garden, a yew labyrinth and a short woodland and pond walk.' The dovecote was not built as such, but formed from the original defences of the house, the structure being built in the 16th century. The date 1641 in the brickwork records the time when Fulke and Margaret Walwyn (hence the associated initials F.M.W.) carried out extensive repair works to the house and adapted this building for use as a dovecote.

5 Hereford
& the ancient capitals and palaces of central Herefordshire

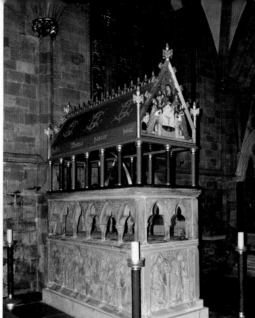

HEREFORD CATHEDRAL

We can't do justice to the cathedral in this book, only give you an indication of things to look for. Much of the structure dates to the Norman period, notably the great round pillars of the nave and much of the fabric of the south transept. The Lady Chapel was added in the late 1100s or first half of the 1200s, and the upper part of the chancel was then rebuilt, followed by a rebuilding of the north transept. The Booth Porch, outside which the walk begins, was built in 1519. The upper parts of the nave were largely rebuilt in the 1780s after the west front had collapsed. Particular points of interest include (in an anti-clockwise direction having entered the cathedral) the Cantilupe Shrine, recently restored, which commemorates St Thomas Cantilupe, bishop of Hereford 1275-1282, who was canonised after his death as the result of miracles performed at his tomb (above centre); the Stanbury chapel with its fan vaulting and stained glass which shows how the cathedral appeared before the collapse of the west front (above left); the crypt with its tombstone to Phillips, cider-maker; the Lady Chapel with the Audley Chapel on its southern side (above right) in which you will find modern stained glass by Tom Denny inspired by the writing of Thomas Traherne, and scattered around, a number of tombs and monuments – and not forgetting the Mappa Mundi exhibition and the Chained Library, on the other side of the shop and café.

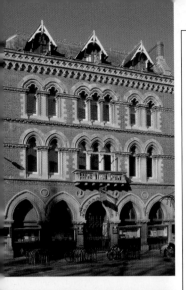

BUILDINGS OF BROAD STREET

Looking up the street from the cathedral end, on the left is Hereford Library and Museum. This was built in the 1870s from a range of types of stone found across southern Britain; the designer's aim was to represent the sediments of the Earth upon which the living world exists, illustrated on the façade by carvings of both plants and animals. The building has been described as an example of 'Anglicised Venetian Gothic'. The exhibits explore the history, social history and natural history of the county and include Roman mosaics, a colony of bees, swords, costumes, textiles and fine art. For details of opening times check www.herefordshire.gov.uk/history-lives/hereford-museums-art-gallery.

On the right is St Francis Xavier Roman Catholic church, where you can see the shrine that contains the hand of St John Kemble. Kemble was born in 1599 into a prominent Catholic family in south Herefordshire, an area where Catholicism remained comparatively strong as it did in neighbouring parts of Monmouthshire. He was ordained a priest on the Continent, and in 1625 returned to Herefordshire, where he carried out his religious duties, being based for most of the next 50 years at Pembridge Castle (near Welsh Newton) on which his brother had taken a lease. His peaceful existence was shattered in 1678 when the fabricated Popish Plot, which proposed to replace Charles II with his Catholic brother James, was 'uncovered' by Titus Oates. John Kemble was caught up in the flurry of subsequent accusations, taken to London and tried. He was found innocent of any involvement in the plot, but sentenced to death on the treasonous grounds of being a Catholic priest. He was returned to Hereford where the sentence of hanging, drawing and quartering was carried out on Widemarsh Common. He was canonized in 1970.

Further on on the left is the Green Dragon Hotel, its Georgian façade masking a range of earlier buildings including a fine 17th-century timber-framed house; the Green Dragon was once one of the city's main coaching inns. On the right is Barclays Bank, once the City Arms, another major coaching inn. Notice the dip in the bank's ground-floor window-sills: this reflects that the buildings here are built across the line of the old Saxon ditch that once surrounded a smaller Hereford, the buildings settling into the less well consolidated ground of the infilled ditch.

All Saints church, at the end of Broad Street, dates mainly to the Early English period in the late 1200s, with some later Decorated windows and tracery. It now serves as both church and café. There is a Jacobean pulpit and a set of misericords.

The west face of the cathedral now stands one bay to the east of its original position, the nave being shortened after the collapse of 1786, and was rebuilt by James Wyatt. In 1902-8 it was replaced by the current façade designed by John Oldrid Scott. Join the road here and turn right along Broad Street towards All Saints church.

2 Turn right into the High Street and carry on ahead briefly into High Town. As you enter this paved area, look out for the stone in the ground that commemorates the spot where Owen Tudor – who married Henry V's widowed queen, their grandson becoming Henry VII – was executed after the Battle of Mortimers Cross (for which see pp.44-5). According to one description, Owen's head was washed, his hair and beard combed by 'a madwoman', and then the head was displayed on top of the market cross. His body is believed subsequently to have been buried in the Greyfriars (the site of which you'll pass later in the walk), but both the Greyfriars and any grave have long since disappeared.

Turn away from High Town for the moment and walk down Widemarsh Street to the ring road, to pass through the site of Widemarsh Gate in the city walls, which was demolished in the 1890s. On the right is the Farmers Club, a listed building dating back to the 17th century. In 1865 it was established as a boys' school attended by the young Alfred Watkins, and from 1926 till early in the new millennium it was a private members' club.

INNS OF WIDEMARSH STREET
Opposite the entrance to Maylord Street is the Imperial, the inn to which Charles Watkins, founder of the Imperial Brewery at the rear of the site and father of Alfred Watkins of photographic and ley line fame, moved in 1847. On the opposite side of the road, on the corner with Maylord Street furthest from the town centre, once stood the Angel Inn. It was here that the actor David Garrick was born in 1717, his father, a captain in the army, then being in the city on a recruiting tour. The inn burnt down in the early 19th century and was replaced by the current building.

CONINGSBY HOSPITAL

This was founded as a home for old soldiers by Sir Thomas Coningsby c.1614 on the site of a house that had belonged to the Knights Templar, parts of which survive in the north range. The large gateway initially led to Sir Thomas's house, which was built behind the hospital on the site of the cloister of Blackfriars' monastery. The residents used to wear red coats and it is believed that the hospital led to the founding of the Chelsea Hospital, thanks to local girl Nell Gwynne who became a 'favourite' of Charles II and who is known to have supported the Chelsea Hospital. (The museum here, which tells the story of the hospital as well as containing information about the Templars, Hospitallers and Crusades, is currently open from April to October on Wednesday and Saturday between 11am and 3pm, but best to check on 01432 274903.)

BLACKFRIARS

The Black Friars or Dominicans established a presence in Hereford from c.1246, on a site to the west of the current one. Their presence was not looked upon favourably by the cathedral clergy in the 1270s, but in 1319 Edward II granted them a new site alongside that granted by Sir John Daniel, the then bishop adding a further grant. Daniel was executed in 1321 but the friars were adept at acquiring adjacent parcels of land and built up a sizeable acreage in the vicinity on which they constructed their monastery and laid out gardens and orchards. Edward III was present at the dedication of the new building. Several notable people chose to be buried here, including the earl of Pembroke in 1376 and the bishop of Chester (who had died in Hereford) in 1394. In 1352 there was a prior and eleven brethren; numbers had fallen to seven brethren by the time of the Dissolution.

Cross over the ring road and keep walking along Widemarsh Street till you come to the Coningsby Hospital on the right-hand side. Take the path to the right of the hospital (as you look at its front) to find the remains of the Blackfriars monastery and its preaching cross.

3 Head back down the path to Widemarsh Street and turn left back towards the city centre. Take the first left (Coningsby Street) and walk along to its end, crossing over Monkmoor Street/Canal Street into a graveyard. Walk along the path through this to Commercial Road, looking out for the grave to John Venn (which is surrounded by railings), and also the memorial gate to his sister at the far end of the graveyard.

JOHN VENN

Having trained as an Anglican priest, John Venn was appointed to the living of St Peter's in Hereford in 1833 and never left. His parish was one of the poorest parts of the city, and he soon began organising a soup kitchen. However, believing that poverty could be overcome through work, he was at the forefront of founding the Society for Aiding the Industrious, which is still active in Hereford. The Society created a hive of activity in the Portfields area between Bath Street and the current hospital. They built and ran a steam corn mill, and a baths complex and swimming pool which was heated by waste energy from the mill. They established allotments and created a model farm, and bought coal in bulk in summer so they could pass on cheaper prices in winter.

THE BLACK AND WHITE HOUSE

Built in 1621, it is the only surviving building of what was the Butchers Row and Cooken Row. For many years it was a butcher's, then a saddler's and a hardware shop before becoming a branch of Lloyd's Bank. They gave it to Hereford City Council in 1928, since when it has been a museum. Furnished in Jacobean style, it has relics of the Civil War, several rare wall paintings and a model of the medieval city showing the full circuit of the walls. It is open for limited hours every day except Monday, but best to check www.herefordshire.gov.uk//history-lives/hereford-museums-art-gallery.

BODENHAM LAKE NATURE RESERVE

The area of the lake was once fields that formed part of Lady Close Farm, but from the 1920s was given over to quarrying gravel. In 1994 Leominster District Council (now subsumed into Herefordshire Council) bought the site to retain it for recreation and conservation, and it is now managed by the Herefordshire Wildlife Trust. The reserve covers 110 acres and includes the largest body of open water in the county, as well as meadows, old and new orchards, and an area of wet woodland. Half the site has no public access, but you can stroll in the orchards and meadows and visit a bird hide. More than 160 species of birds have been recorded here (including goosander, smew, teal and wigeon), and otters have been seen too.

❸ Some 25 yards past the entrance to the Railway Inn on the far side of the bridge, take the path on your right, which starts by ascending a set of steps and then heads on straight up the hillside. The path passes to the right of a house and then emerges onto the A49.

❹ Turn right and cross the road (take very good care) in the vicinity of the driveway entrance to Queenswood Cottage, some 30 yards along on the far side of the road. Once across the A49 continue following the road, looking out for any suitable path on your left to reach a path that shadows the A49 within Queenswood Arboretum. Wherever you reach this path, turn right on it and keep turning right at subsequent junctions, and the network of paths will bring you (via some redwoods; look out for bears and

200

EATON CAMP

This hillfort has natural defences to the north in the Wye and to the south-east with the valley of the Cage Brook. Excavations in 2012 showed that the west-facing ramparts that cut off the promontory on which this Iron Age hillfort sits probably date to *c.*350-300BC and superseded a line of ditch and bank constructed further to the east some 100 or 200 years earlier. Further excavations in 2013 showed that there was a bank around the outer side of the tip of the promontory in the Iron Age and provided evidence of a round-house with a carefully surfaced interior floor. They also located a deep pit or shaft that was not excavated. The main entrance to the hillfort was probably at the north-west corner.

field. Here the path turns left to pass between the ramparts of the hillfort and some buildings screened by a high fence. The path then heads down to the banks of the Wye, and follows this, before starting to head uphill while still following the Wye. When you reach a wooden gate behind which a flight of steps leads up to a long narrow building (until relatively recently the Camp or Ancient Camp Inn, and before that a shop and a blacksmith's), turn right down the steps towards the Wye, turning left near the bottom to emerge into a field via a stile. Stay close to the Wye through this field, crossing a small bridge at the far end, beyond which the path stays between the fence of the next field and the Wye. The path soon passes alongside an island near the end of which it enters a field.

WYE SSSI

Populations of native crayfish, otter and two rare fish, the twaite and allis shad, have contributed to the river's selection as a Site of Special Scientific Interest. From Hay on Wye to Bredwardine, the river flows over sandstone, mudstone and hard limestone, while from Bredwardine to Holme Lacy it meanders across a broad floodplain of clay over sandstone through rich agricultural land. The river bed is mostly gravelly with currents ranging from fast in shallow runs to sluggish in the deeper pools. The Wye is noted for its floating water-crowfoot species. The larvae of many insects such as mayflies, stoneflies and dragonflies support an outstanding assemblage of unionid mussels (a freshwater or river mussel), a declining population of the rare freshwater pearl mussel and a population of the native Atlantic stream crayfish that has been little affected by crayfish plague. The Wye is considered to be the best salmon river in England and a further 28 fish species have been recorded. Birds which feed on insects and fish in the rivers and streams include kingfisher, goosander, cormorant, dipper and yellow wagtail. Recent increases in phosphate levels from sewage and agricultural run off, combined with the spread of the invasive species of Himalayan Balsam and Japanese Knotweed, are severely affecting the river.

4 Turn left along the edge of the field and after some 40 yards bear left up the track to the left of a house, the track leading to a tarmacked lane. Follow this lane, which will bend right and then left, to a T-junction. Here, turn left to return to Eaton Bishop, turning right in the village to return to the church.

Walk 32
Kilpeck

6.5 miles, largely on woodland and field paths, the Herefordshire Trail, minor roads and tracks. A few stiles. Includes a church, deserted medieval village site, a castle with some stonework and The Mynde.

Park in the car park by the church (GR 445 305).

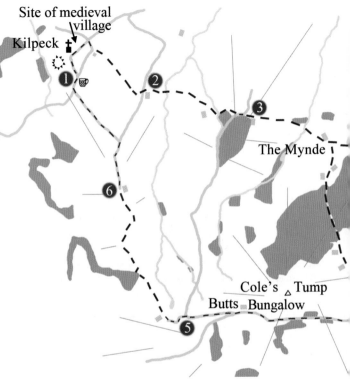

❶ Having visited the church (see pp.221-2) and castle (see pp.228-9), turn left out of the churchyard and walk along the road with the site of the medieval village on your left until you reach a crossroads. Turn right here and at the bend you quickly reach, carry on ahead down a track, initially passing a red brick structure on your right. Before you reach the next field, which is very large, the path technically crosses a stile on your left, then follows the hedgeline (now on your right) to cross a footbridge into the large field. (If obstructed, you may find it easier to use the field gateway and reach the end of the footbridge by then turning left. It may be that the farmer has not reinstated the footpaths across the next fields, in which case you may decide to follow the field boundaries on your right or any tramlines across the fields.) From the end of the footbridge the path heads straight across this field to a

stile, over which you head across the next field, aiming for an internal corner of the field on the skyline, to the right of a house. From this internal corner of the field, follow the field boundary on your right till you reach a footpath sign just before you reach the house, where you cross out of the field through a gate onto a road.

THE HEREFORDSHIRE SCHOOL OF ROMANESQUE SCULPTURE

Two leading master craftsmen have been identified as the men essentially responsible for the work of this school of sculpture that was active predominantly but not exclusively in Herefordshire (there are examples of the work in Radnorshire, Shropshire, Worcestershire and Gloucestershire) in the 1130s and early 1140s. The sources of inspiration are many and varied. The *Bestiary*, the Book of Beasts derived from the Greek *Physiologus* which was translated into Latin in the 5th century, is considered the primary source. This gives shape to many mythical beasts, to which have been added elements of Celtic, Anglo-Saxon and Romano-British styles, enriched by encounters with sculptures seen on the pilgrimage trail to Santiago de Compostela. The master craftsmen seem to have received their training at Hereford Cathedral, where forerunners of the work of the Herefordshire School can be seen. Typical features of the School include the ribbed draperies in which figures are clothed, egg-shaped human heads with large bulging eyes, large open hands with long fingers, beaded medallions joined by masks, birds carved in profile, male figures with large feet, one bird pecking the head of another, thick serpentine bodies with heads that have large eyes and gaping mouths, quadrupeds with one front leg raised with a drooping paw, and symmetrical and asymmetrical knots. After Shobdon (see Walk 6), Kilpeck had the greatest range of the school's work; other churches have sculpture perhaps confined to a doorway or the font. (Both Shobdon and Kilpeck had comparatively wealthy patrons.) When looking at this work it is extraordinary to reflect that this artistic enterprise was taking shape during the Anarchy, the wars between King Stephen and Henry I's declared heiress, Matilda.

KILPECK CHURCH

The church has been described as one of the most perfect Norman village churches; the addition of the belfry and an internal gallery are the only major changes to have been made to it since its construction. (There is also a possible survival from an earlier Saxon church in a section of long and short work on what would have been the corner of a building, now visible on the outside wall at the north-east corner of the nave.) The sculpture embellishes the south doorway and includes an exterior corbel table running round the whole church together with dragon heads protruding from the west wall and decoration to the west window and to the chancel arch; the massive font is left undecorated.

The left jamb of the doorway has two knights entwined in plant-like stems and two serpents, its capital having a basilisk (a mythical beast hatched from a cock's egg by a serpent) and a lion clawing at each other. On the right of the door are carved foliage and doves, the capital bearing a human head from whose mouth flows more foliage. The arch contains a carving of an angel at the apex, with, to its left, a phoenix. Other carvings include dragons and grotesque heads, a manticore (human-headed lion), birds, the sign of Pisces and various forms of foliage.

The corbel table represents a wide variety of human life and its function seems to have been both to entertain and to educate about good and evil. There are several carvings of human beings, and of heads with leonine features that may represent aspects of human behaviour; one with a bowl to its mouth, for example, may represent gluttony. Carvings of stags, fish, horses and the hound and the hare may reflect life on the lord's manor – and it was the lord who was paying for this work. There is a corbel of two entwined serpents, two of pigs' heads (one with a human head to the side), some of rams, a sheela-na-gig and a fiddle player (each representing low morals), an ibex (it appears to us upside down, but the *Bestiary* relates how an ibex's horns supported it if it fell down a mountain), two fledgling birds, two of an Agnus Dei, a pair of dancers that seem to warn against seduction, and others of Celtic and Saxon-style interlace, and many more. The chancel arch has carvings of figures including one of St Peter, whilst the boss in the centre of the apse is carved with four cats' masks biting the joining ribs.

2 Turn left on the road and almost immediately right up some steps and over a stile into a field by the side of the house. Follow the hedge that forms the boundary of the house's garden and when this turns right, continue on the same line that you've just been walking, down the slope to a footbridge across the stream in the valley bottom. Cross the bridge and carry on up the next slope, still on roughly the same line, to pass through the hedge on the ridge ahead. Once through the hedgeline, turn slightly right to head across the next field aiming slightly to the left of a group of farm buildings in trees which will come into view as you cross the field. In due course you'll see a small gate in the hedgeline ahead; head for this and pass through it. On roughly the same line, head across the next field towards a bridge near the far corner which crosses the stream in the valley bottom. Over this bridge, follow the edge of the woodland on your right up the next slope and when you reach the corner of woodland in about 100 yards, bear half-right across the field on a line to the right of two oak trees to a gate which leads you onto a road. (Once again, it may prove easier to follow the field boundaries on this stretch if crops obstruct the path.)

3 Go almost straight across the road to a stile and cross this to follow the edge of a wood on your right to cross another stile to the right of a new barn and head towards a brick-built house. Turn left and then right on the gravel tracks to walk around the edge of the property keeping it just to your right, to cross a stile just to the left

ST ANN'S WELL & LADY WELL

Washing in the waters of St Ann's Well is said to cure various ills, particularly eye troubles. The first bucketful of water collected after Twelfth Night was supposed to be the best, the water in the pool to the north-east of the well bubbling up at midnight.

The Lady Well is a spring which is haunted by the ghost of a young woman who killed herself there. In another more elaborate version of the story she killed her lover, wrongly suspecting him of infidelity, then died of heartbreak beside the well, haunting the spot ever afterwards.

ACONBURY HILLFORT

A single rampart follows the contour of the hill to enclose an area of about 17.5 acres, with the steepest slopes away from the fort on the north and west, the ditch surviving on the south and east sides and largely infilled on the others. There were two original entrances, one in the south-east corner where each rampart turns in, and one in the south-west corner where one rampart curls behind the other. Other gaps in the defences are probably later openings. A survey in 1951 produced evidence of occupation, including a large amount of Iron Age pottery. Some Roman pottery was also found. In 1642 the hillfort was briefly occupied by Lord Herbert for the Royalists in the Civil War and in 1645 it was occupied and strengthened by the Scottish army besieging Hereford under the earl of Leven.

❸ Turn right on the road. Having passed a wood on your left, the road bends first left and then right. Past this second bend, when you reach a field gate on your right, if you look into the field you will see a line of trees and bushes to the left. At the right-hand end of these is the site of St Ann's Well. Further along the road you come to a pond on your right, one source of its water supply being the Lady Well which is sited up the hillside from here, close to the edge of the wood. Keep following the road to Aconbury church.

❹ Once you've visited the church, return up the road, and just past the bend between the farm buildings on the right and Aconbury Court on the left, go through the footpath gate on your left. The path slants downhill to go through another gate to join a track that crosses a small

ACONBURY PRIORY

A priory of nuns was founded here early in the 13th century by Margaret, wife of William de Lacy, who had founded Craswall priory. She managed to encourage King John to grant a tract of land to support the nunnery in 1216 (see ACONBURY WOODS overleaf), and the church was built c.1230-40. Margaret decided that the nunnery should be attached to the Hospitaller preceptory at Dinmore, but she hadn't appreciated that members of the Order were liable for service overseas. She approached the pope to see if instead the nunnery could be turned into one for Austin canons, but the Hospitallers objected, resulting in lengthy arguments that lasted for five years (and are believed to have cost Margaret the substantial sum of 600 marks in fees) before Margaret's wishes were acted upon, probably in the late 1230s. In 1354 an illegitimate nun was allowed to become prioress following a special dispensation.

It is not known what part, if any, of the church belonged to the parish. The structure is essentially Norman, but is usually locked as it is no longer used for regular services. On the nunnery's suppression in 1536, when there were seven nuns, the conventual buildings were demolished, leaving slight traces of the western range, where it adjoined the church's south side, including some springers for the stone arches and corbels to support floors. High on the wall near the western end is an archway with a square squint looking into the church that would have been used by invalids unable to attend the services. Two early doorways, now walled up, gave access to the church from this side, one to the nave and the other to the chancel. The porch was added late in the 15th century. The church was restored in the early 1700s by James Brydges, Lord Chandos, who made a vault underneath the church where he was buried in 1714. The church was again restored in 1863.

The field surrounding the churchyard has signs of banks, hollows and platforms which may indicate sites of buildings or boundary walls. A seemingly man-made bank about two feet high and five feet wide leads away from the nearby brook at right angles; it may have been a causeway running through the boggy ground to a bridge that connected this area, then possibly quarries, to the priory.

ACONBURY WOODS

Aconbury was part of the Norman Royal Forest, its first mention being in 1213 when King John licensed the taking of 33 oaks from the woods for repairs to Hereford Castle. Three years later he granted roughly 360 acres (three caracutes) of the woods which were to be cleared and farmed in support of the new nunnery. In 1257 further royal grants allowed the nunnery to use the woods for pasturing stock without payment of the usual penalties. At the dissolution of the nunnery, Henry VIII retained the right to sell large timber, but allowed smaller timber to be sold by John Scudamore of Wilton. In 1573 the woods were described in a legal case which referred to extensive coppicing as well as significant depredations to young trees caused by rabbits, resulting in large areas becoming open pasture. In 1641 the Brydges family, subsequently dukes of Chandos, acquired the manor of Aconbury and with it the woods. They sold their Herefordshire estates to the Trustees of Guy's Hospital in London in 1731. The woodland unaffected by the rabbits (whose damage seem to have been focused on the southern slopes) continued to be coppiced on a 15 to 20 year cycle. Gradually the activity became uneconomic and in about the 1830s the area was replanted with trees.

stream near the foot of a pond. Follow the track round to the right along the edge of the pond, and then a field boundary. Follow the track into the woodland and then keep ahead to follow the track uphill. You will meet a forestry track which you cross to continue now steeply uphill. Keep to the main path and when you reach a T-junction of paths near the top of the hill, turn right. At another junction soon reached, turn left and this path will lead you to a stile that leads out onto a minor road.

5 Cross the road and go over the stile into the field. Here the path turns slightly to the right and crosses the field, heading towards a couple of cottages on the skyline of the next ridge. Leave the field by a footpath gate next to a telegraph pole, cross the farm lane and go over another stile into the next field. The path crosses this on a line slightly to the left of that you have just been taking, to head for the far top corner. Here you leave the field by a stile and turn right onto a sunken lane. This, via a few bends, will lead you to a gate opposite a house. Go through the gate and turn right on the lane, following this across the end of a tarmacked road and then bearing left just in front of an intriguingly-shaped end wall of a house. Follow this lane over a crossroads of roads and tracks and down a path to join a minor road.

6 Turn right on this and pass the Castle Inn. From the pub, keep walking uphill along the road, following it round the sharp bend soon reached. Eventually, opposite High View Cottage, you will reach a right turn along a small lane; turn right along here, and then right again to return to the village hall and your car.

Walk 34
Mordiford
& Backbury Hillfort

4.5 miles, largely on tracks, field edge and woodland paths, and minor roads. Some stiles. Includes a hillfort, and you can also visit Mordiford church.

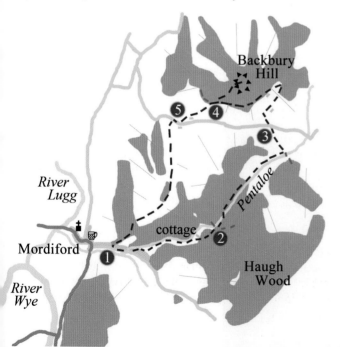

MORDIFORD

You may want to wander down to the Lugg and the church at the start or end of your walk. The bridge which crosses the Lugg here, just up from its confluence with the Wye, was built in 1352, though much repaired in the 15th and 16th centuries. Until 1811 the church had a green dragon some 12 feet long painted on its west end. Though this probably represented the Wyvern on the arms of the priory of St Guthlac, which had held the living of Mordiford, it served as a reminder of a local piece of folklore concerning a dragon which used to devour animals and humans in the neighbourhood. Nobody was willing to attempt to kill it until a condemned criminal hid in a barrel at the dragon's favourite drinking spot. The barrel, as with many such stories, was barbed with knives and pike blades so that when the dragon smelled the potential human meal inside and fastened on it, the beast severely wounded itself. In the ensuing struggle, both man and dragon were killed. Of the church building, the south doorway is Norman, the tower was built in 1811 (replacing one that formerly stood at the junction of the nave and chancel), and the north aisle was added in the 19th century.

In Mordiford take the minor road east off the B4224, signposted Checkley, and after a few hundred yards, park in a sort of layby on the left, just before a stream is culverted under the road and before you reach a steep '10% hill' road sign (GR 574 373).

1 Walk on up the road and where it bends slightly to the right, take the footpath off to the left. This leads round some houses and onto another road. Walk along this road and after the third bungalow on the left, take the footpath that heads between two bungalows, this quickly leading you out into a shallow valley clad by woods on either side. Walk up this valley, the path initially keeping close to the stream on your left, then crossing to the woods on the right-hand side where it joins a track on which you turn left. This track then takes you back to the left-hand side of the valley and in due course to a fence in front of a ruined cottage. Walk along this fence with the cottage on your left and pass through a gate at the far end into the woodland. Walk up into the woodland and in a few yards you meet a track up some steps. Turn left on the track and follow this along the valley, it presently meeting another track which your route crosses to pick up a footpath that stays close to the stream on your left.

CHASE HILL HILLFORT

Chase Hill was occupied during the Mesolithic and Bronze Age, but it was during the Iron Age in the 4th or 5th century BC that the earthworks were extended to encompass an area of some 27 acres that was home to perhaps 1,400 people. It is possible that this expansion occurred at a time when the Malverns were the centre of a large pottery industry. Many of the 'defences' were formed by scarping the natural slope, but on the south side a bank was constructed which still stands some 5½ feet high.

⑤ Continue on the track to the left of the farm and crossing the farm's access lane, enter Merrivale Nature Reserve through a kissing gate. At a junction of paths soon reached, bear right and carry on through the wood to leave it by a kissing gate near a stone bench. Walk straight on (there's a wire fence on your right), then turn

---

ALTON COURT

There has probably been a dwelling here since the 13th century, but the present house was built in the second half of the 16th century to a half H-shaped plan, with parts subsequently modernised and rebuilt. The end of the north-west wing retains its close studding and herringbone timbering, indicative that it was high status building when first erected. Thomas Blake, a Ross resident and philanthropist, acquired the house and estate in the 1880s so that he could construct a series of reservoirs and associated waterworks to improve the town's water supply, with water being pumped to another reservoir at the Prospect (see below).

---

left at a large oak tree, following the Wye Valley Walk down towards Ross. At a crossroads of paths, go straight ahead through a metal gate, then turn left and head down the field. At the bottom of the field, turn left and go through a metal kissing gate (still following the Wye Valley Walk). You will emerge on a lane (Penyard Lane) outside Alton Court.

⑥ Walk down Penyard Lane, turning left into a road (Gresleys), opposite a sign for Penyard Lane, and just before the entrance to the Enterprise Park on the right. At the end of Gresleys, turn left into Merrivale Lane, then after 40 yards right onto a footpath. When this meets a road on the right (Sussex Avenue), turn right, heading for the church. Go straight on at a crossroads to pass a green on the right. Cross the main road ahead and carry straight on (Old Maids Walk), and cross into the churchyard and the Prospect. Return to the Market Hall via the Plague Cross, dropping down to the road in front of Rudhall's Almshouses, on which you turn left.

ROSS-ON-WYE CHURCH

The earliest surviving stonework of the church dates to the 1280s, but most of the structure is later. The tower was built in the 14th century, when the chancel was extended and the north porch built. The nave was raised in 1743. The church is notable for its collection of monuments, including alabaster effigies of various members of the Rudhall family. The east window was brought here from the bishop's palace at Stretton Sugwas and dates to the 15th century.

250

a T-junction. Cross the junction and take the bridleway in the field ahead, which follows the field boundaries on your right. This very soon bends to the left, then to the right further along, and having crossed a field boundary, through a footpath gate, now follow a hedgerow on your left and pass an isolated copse in a field on your right. As you near another tongue of woodland on your right, and reach another field boundary, cross the stile on your left and walk up the left-hand side of the hedgerow, to meet a track at the far end of the field, which is also the Wye Valley Walk. Turn left on the track, and follow it to the next field junction, where you turn sharp right and follow the field boundary on your left up to a minor road.

7 Turn left on the road and walk along past a few cottages till, after about a third of a mile, you come to a car park and picnic area on the right. Immediately before this, take the track off to the right which slants downhill towards the Wye. Keep the Wye on your left and walk past quarries on your right and then up a track to meet a road. Turn right on the road and follow this up to the

259

CAPLER CAMP

This long, thin, oval-shaped hillfort covers an area of around 15.5 acres (including the ramparts). The ramparts vary in strength and complexity. Those above the steep slopes to the north consist of ditches dug into the hillside, while on the gentler slopes to the south there is a double rampart. The original entrances were on the eastern and south-western sides. Excavations were carried out in 1924, before many of the archaeological techniques used today had been adopted. The excavations found some worked flints and a Roman bronze coin, but no evidence for any structures, though they might have overlooked such evidence. The soil here is very acidic and might in any event have dissolved much of any pottery, ironwork or bone objects left by any inhabitants.

crest of the hill, where, just before a house on the left, you take a track off to the left, which is again part of the Wye Valley Walk. This leads up towards the ramparts of Capler Camp. Before you reach them, take the signposted path which makes a half-right turn through a small conifer plantation, on the far side of which you emerge by the ramparts.

8 The path now turns right to follow the ramparts, then follows the Wye Valley Walk to pass through a gate and follow a route in what would have been the ditch between the two ramparts. The path (and ramparts) bend to the left and you pass a stone barn on your right, immediately after which you leave the Wye Valley Walk, turning right onto the track along the hill crest, passing another obelisk on your right and a trig point on your left to reach a gate out onto a lane. Turn right on the lane and walk along the drive of a house, keeping the house to your left and some outbuildings to your right to enter a field beyond. The path crosses this field to the far side, passes through a kissing-gate, and in the next field, which has another obelisk, drops to a stile in the lower hedgerow (the left-hand stile of two). Across the stile the path heads across the field to another obelisk next to a stile. Cross this and then cross the field, aiming for the right-hand side of a house with a conservatory. Head through the field gate to the right of the house and walk down the lane to the road ahead, joining it near a BT phone box. Turn right on the lane to return to Brockhampton church.

Walk 37
Hoarwithy, King's Caple, Sellack & Llanfrother

6.25 miles, largely on grassland and field paths, minor roads and tracks. Some stiles. Includes three churches, a castle motte and the site of a Celtic monastery.

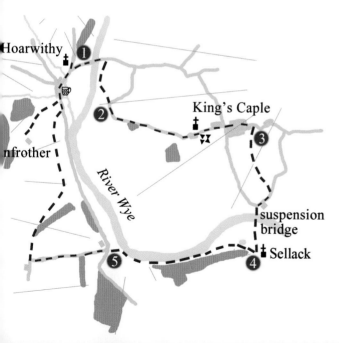

Park by the church in Hoarwithy (see p.266) (GR 546 294).

1 For the walk, take the road towards King's Caple and cross the river Wye. Notice the old tollhouse on the right.

> **HOARWITHY TOLL BRIDGE**
> A bridge was first built here after the passing of the 1855 Hoarwithy Bridge Act. It opened two years later and tolls were collected until 1835 when Herefordshire County Council took over responsibility for the bridge. The cottage was let out till 2007, when it was sold.

Once over the bridge, turn right on the wide track that is signposted almost immediately and follows the left bank of the Wye. Stay on the track which before long bears away to join a road.

2 Keep straight ahead on the road and it will gradually lead you uphill to King's Caple church and castle mound. Carry on past the church, past the 18th-century King's Caple Court with its parapet and central pediment and across the road junction ahead, looking out for the old school building of 1840 on the right. This ceased to be a school in 1902 when the current school was opened, and the building is now used as a village hall. As you reach the edge of the village, you pass a road junction (with Caple Avenue) on the right and shortly afterwards turn right along a track between High House and some bungalows.

261

KING'S CAPLE CHURCH AND MOTTE

The church is largely in the Decorated style (late 13th to early 14th century) with ballflower ornamentation, but has notable Perpendicular elements in its south porch and north (or Aramstone) chapel. There is a tall Jacobean pulpit with sounding board above, and Jacobean stalls in the chancel, as well as an 18th-century west gallery. The north chapel contains some medieval stained glass, a memorial by John Flaxman (to Mrs Holcombe Ferguson) and another by Sir Richard Westmacott (to Eliza Woodhouse). Outside is an old preaching cross. The motte lies to the south-east of the church and retains some masonry buried in the embankment that runs around its top, indicating that it once had a shell keep. Any trace of a bailey seems to have vanished.

❸ Follow this track and when it reaches a gateway leading to a house, bear right, keeping to the right of a tarmacked drive. Go over the stile at the end of the track and keep to the right of the gate just yards ahead to follow the hedge on your left to a kissing gate. Through the gate, walk across the corner of the field, aiming for the steeple of Sellack church. At the edge of the field, turn left and follow the hedgeline on your right downhill. When this bears right, carry on downhill on the same line to leave the field by a kissing gate. Turn right on the road and when this bends sharply right, take the path off to the left which soon crosses a narrow suspension bridge back across the Wye. On the far side of the bridge, carry on ahead, aiming just to the right of Sellack church.

❷ Once back in woodland, when the road splits bear left on the lane that leads slightly uphill signposted to Home Farm and Glenwye; don't continue on to the youth hostel. This lane passes cottages and farm buildings on your left, and further on starts to follow the wall that encloses Courtfield and the hermitage — in 2021 the wall was being rebuilt and soon it may no longer be possible to see the ruins of the latter.

COURTFIELD

The site is well positioned as a place of relative security protected as it is by a great sweep of the Wye, and various charters indicate that a British king or chief, Custhenin, had a hunting lodge where the house now stands. Some equate Custhenin with a Constantine who was reputed to be the father-in-law of St Dubricius who in turn is credited with 'crowning' King Arthur (see p.265). Was this Constantine the same as Emperor Constantine III who ruled in Britain from 407 to 411? Whatever the facts behind these stories, the site may have a religious significance long before it was the seat of a significant Catholic family.

A mound next to the house is actually a geological feature, but may nevertheless have been used as a castle site. It is certainly believed that the future Henry V, when about 8 years old (he had been born in nearby Monmouth), was cared for here by Lady Margaret Montacute (wife of the earl of Salisbury) after the death of his mother, Mary de Bohun. From some time in the 16th century until 1950 Courtfield was in the ownership of the Vaughans, a staunchly Catholic family. They laid out a park in the 19th century that included several ornamental buildings, of which the hermitage with gothic arches and a single room stands close to the walk. However, elements of the hermitage may date from earlier landscaping; this also included terraces with walls and yew hedges to the south of the current house, which was built in 1805.

Soon after you start to walk along side this wall, you reach a split in the track. At this point the footpath as shown on OS maps has been diverted since the summer of 2012. Take the left-hand track and once you reach the bend ahead (near the remains of a walled garden on your right), continue ahead to a small gate into a field. The diverted path now follows the field boundaries on your right, soon turning to the right round the corner of a small wood and circling round the hill. You pass through one gateway between fields, and at the next field boundary reached (with Courtfield now above you to the right, probably largely shrouded by trees but you might spot its chapel's bell-cote) go through the footpath gate just down from the corner of the field. Once in the next field, turn left to rejoin the 'old' footpath and follow the field boundary on your left down to the river.

❸ Here, turn left on the Wye Valley Path which follows the Wye, keeping on this in a great arc until it eventually heads into some woodland which stretches down to the river. Keep on this path just above the river (ignoring paths off to the left) and in due course you will pass through a footpath gate into a field. Keep following the path above the river to reach Kerne Bridge.

4 Take the steps up on to the road, on which you turn left, passing Flanesford Priory on the far side of the road, with the outline of Goodrich Castle on the skyline beyond. As you approach a bridge across the road, keep to the path alongside the road that rises up to the top of the bridge. Once on the bridge, turn right to return to your vehicle.

You may wish to make two short side trips. That to Goodrich Castle involves turning right at the crossroads and following the road to the castle visitor centre, and then keeping to the footpath beyond to see the outside of the castle. (You'll need to buy tickets at the visitor centre if you want to go in.)

FLANESFORD PRIORY

This was an Augustinian priory founded in 1346 by Richard Talbot, then lord of Goodrich. The Augustinian order discouraged asceticism and encouraged the doing of good works: building and running hospitals, leper colonies and schools, for example. The priory was dissolved in 1536, but its refectory somehow survived subsequent pillaging of the stone for building materials. It now forms the core of a group of holiday apartments and wedding venue.

GOODRICH CASTLE (For opening times check www.english-heritage.org.uk.)
The earliest mention of a castle is in 1101. Who built it is uncertain, but its purpose was clear: to control the ford that crosses the Wye below the castle. The weakest defences are on the side that leads towards the village, and here deep ditches were cut into the rock. The earliest part is the keep, built of a greenish conglomerate, possibly from Coppett Hill, which contrasts with the local red sandstone of the rest of the castle. It passed to William de Valence in the mid 1200s, and under his ownership and that of his son, Aymer, the castle was rebuilt and took the form seen today. It comprises a rectangular curtain wall with semi-circular towers at three corners and a gatehouse tower that also contains the chapel at the fourth. The keep stands in the courtyard so formed. Over subsequent centuries timber buildings were erected abutting the curtain wall, and by the 15th century it had essentially become a large house with a number of small rooms.

By the early 17th century Goodrich had passed to the earls of Kent, and running water was supplied via a long lead pipe that ran across the valley to the west from springs on the opposite hillside. In 1642, Goodrich was garrisoned by Parliamentarian troops but when in December, a large Royalist army approached from south Wales, the castle was evacuated. Not much use was then made of the castle until the spring of 1644 when Henry Lingen, the Royalist Sheriff of Herefordshire, installed a garrison. By August 1644 this numbered over 100 men and horse, and Lingen had fortified the ferryman's house and strewn the ford with caltrops (four-spiked iron balls) to make it impassable by horsemen. Once Colonel Birch had seized Hereford for the Parliamentarians (see p.52), Goodrich became an ever more isolated Royalist outpost. By early 1646 only it and Raglan Castle remained in Royalist hands in the west, and Lingen found himself under siege. Parliamentarian sappers were soon undermining the walls, whilst Birch had cast and brought up a large mortar, Roaring Meg (now on display inside the castle), to pound the buildings inside the curtain wall, after which the Royalists soon surrendered, their position becoming hopeless. In 1647 Parliament ordered that the castle should be slighted, but it had been so badly damaged by Birch's battering that all that was considered necessary was the stripping of lead from any surviving roofs, and it has remained uninhabited ever since.

The other side trip, to Goodrich church, involves turning left at the crossroads and walking down towards the new village school. Turn right on the road that serves the school's car park, to then take the path round the edge of the car park and which then follows the hedge-cum-fence on your left. This leads to a bridge which you cross, the path then following the edge of a field on your left to eventually reach a kissing gate into the churchyard. The church is largely of the Early English and Decorated periods, and has some 15th-century stained glass in the east window of the north aisle.

Walk 39
The Doward

4.5 miles, largely on tracks, the Wye Valley Walk, woodland paths and minor roads. A few stiles. Includes a cave where prehistoric finds have been made, a hillfort, and an ironworking site by the Wye.

Parking in Symonds Yat West is difficult, unless you wish to visit Ye Olde Ferrie Inn, in which case you can use their car park and start the walk at point 4. We have chosen to start from a small parking area near King Arthur's Cave, which means that you could time your walk to arrive at Symonds Yat West (or East if you take a ferry) at lunchtime, although that leaves you with a post-prandial clamber back up the hill.

To reach this parking site, having turned off the A40 to Symonds Yat West, you want to turn onto the road sign-posted to Crocker's Ash that parallels the A40, keeping on it past the petrol station into the settlement of Crocker's Ash. Here, turn left on a minor road signposted 'Doward', 'Biblins' and 'Doward Park Campsite' (in brown). Follow this road as it snakes uphill. After just over a mile the road passes through woodland, and the 'beaten earth' parking area (for about three vehicles) is soon found on the right-hand side, just before a track that slopes away

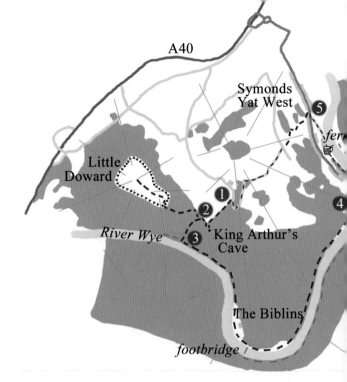

downhill (GR 546 156). (It's just before Doward Park campsite, so if you reach this you've gone too far.)

❶ The walk starts down this track, quickly reaching an information board on the right which gives an account of the natural history and the several nature reserves in the area. The track soon enters an old quarry, at the entrance to which the track turns right. You now pass a

DOWARD WOODLAND

The larger trees are a mixture of ash, beech and oak, with an understorey that includes hazel, field maple, spurge laurel, hawthorn, spindle, guelder rose, whitebeam and yew. The more open areas are dominated by bramble, with abundant dog's mercury. Other plants include bluebells, wood spurge, woodruff, ramsons (wild garlic) and pendulous sedge. Secondary woodland of ash and silver birch has developed through regeneration over the former industrial areas where the exposed rock has become home to shade-loving ferns like hart's tongue, common spleenwort, and the local maidenhair fern. In autumn the area is good for searching out fungi.

INDUSTRY NEAR THE START OF THE WALK

The underlying rock here is carboniferous limestone, which was extensively quarried in the past. By the early 20th century there was a large limestone crusher in the vicinity and two buildings, one for the engine that powered the crusher and the other a manager's office and workers' canteen. The crusher took limestone from nearby quarries.

series of caves on your left, King Arthur's Cave being the main one, found at the point where you are adjacent to the corner of the field that you've been following on your right. If you can't see this through summer foliage, there is a large clear 'platform' outside the cave entrance.

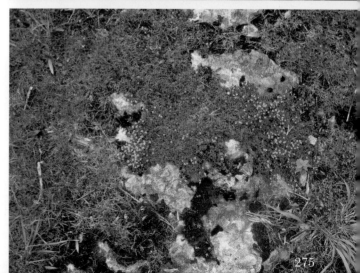

4 Turn right and walk along the lane. You will spot the access path to the ferry that crosses to the Saracens Head in Symonds Yat East. Keep on the road till you reach Ye Old Ferrie Inn, where you can drop down the steps if you want to visit the hostelry. The walk carries on along the lane (or follow the access road that serves the inn if you've dropped in for some sustenance and turn right at its top.) Just past the well-signed entrance to the Paddocks Hotel, you want to take the path off to the left up a series of steps, just this side of a telephone box and Bluebell Cottage. Prepare for some panting!

5 Climb the steps, and when the path splits, take the left-hand fork along the hillside. This will lead you out onto a tarmacked area; cross this and continue on the footpath up the hillside. When you meet a tarmacked lane, turn left. At the junction with driveways soon reached, turn right and immediately left on one of the driveways, and then immediately right again up a path marked with a yellow arrow. This soon passes close by a cottage on your left; at the fork in the path ahead, take the left-hand option. At the next fork, take the right-hand path (again hopefully following the yellow arrow). You will emerge on a concrete track on which you turn left to soon reach a crossroads of tracks and paths. Go straight on up the path between the tree and the hedgerow; the path curves around a white-painted house to join a driveway. Follow this uphill to where it meets a road. Turn left on the 'main' road (i.e. not the no-through road which also leads off left) and follow this back to your vehicle.

Walk 40
Llangarron

4.25 miles, largely on paths across fields (often pasture) or alongside field boundaries, minor roads and tracks. Some stiles. Includes a church and two mansions, one of which, Langstone Court, or at least its gardens, it may be possible to visit (see p.285).

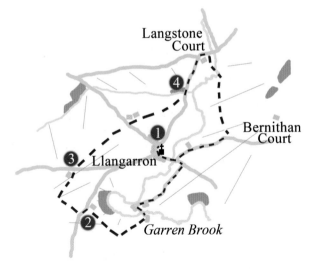

LLANGARRON CHURCH

The church tower and chancel date from the 14th century, but much of the rest of the structure is due to an extensive restoration in 1841 that saw the addition of the large north aisle. There is a fine font of the Perpendicular period, and a tomb cover of a young child is mounted on a wall.

Park in the car park by the church (GR 530 213).

❶ Go through the gates by the car park into the church-yard. Walk through the graveyard down to the bottom corner, and walk out onto the road through a gate and down some steps. Turn left on the road and cross the river, after which you almost immediately turn right onto a smaller road, and then after about 100 yards right onto an even smaller road. Keep on this till its end, past some converted stone barns and an old mill building. At the road's end, just across a river and in front of a set of farm buildings, turn right onto a track which soon narrows to a path. Keep right on this when another path is indicated going straight ahead over a stile, and follow it till it meets a road, the last few yards being on a gravelled lane to the left of some houses.

❷ Turn left on the road and after 50 yards right over a stile onto a footpath which initially follows the field boundary on your left. Soon after passing a large oak in this field boundary, rather than keeping to the boundary, the path carries on ahead aiming at a point roughly half-way between a telegraph pole in the boundary on the left and the first pole in the field on the right, towards a stile that will become visible as you crest the slope. (Depending upon any crop that is obstructing your passage across the field, you may wish to keep to the field boundary and follow it to the end, and then along the top to reach the stile.) Cross the stile onto the lane on the far side, on which you turn right. When you reach a house straight ahead, follow the footpath to its right (following the yellow footpath sign) and walk down to meet a road.

3 Cross the road onto the track on the far side, and follow this along, it later becoming more of a path before it meets another road. Cross this road and go up the bank on the far side to pass to the right of some corrugated sheds. Before you reach the road beyond, the path goes through a gate on your right into a field. Once in the field, turn left to follow the field boundary on your left. A hundred yards or so past the last of the houses on your left you come to a stile in this field boundary which you cross. The path then heads slightly down and across the slope, aiming for the right-hand end of a line of poplars in the valley bottom, crossing one stile and then heading for the far bottom corner of the next field where you cross out onto a road. As you walk across these fields keep an eye out for the red brick Bernithan Court on the hillside across the valley and slightly to your right: this could be the clearest view you have of the building.

4 Turn left on the road and follow it uphill and round Langstone Court on your right. Just past the entrance drive to the Court, and just before you reach the river, take the footpath off to the right through the parkland with its many well-established trees. The path initially passes to the right of a small castellated stone building, then turns left to reach the corner of the parkland made by a bend in the river. There, go through a kissing gate, then along an embankment and over a bridge above a weir and so into a field on the far side of the river.

LANGSTONE COURT

This house, built of brick with ashlar dressings, incorporates an earlier house (of which some of the timber-frame has been retained) that belonged to the Gwillym family of Fawley. The house and neighbouring farmhouse were sold in 1794 to Revd Thomas Jones; the house has stayed in his family ever since, though the farmhouse was sold in 1954. The house, which retains much original panelling and plasterwork, is open to the public several days a year, and the garden as a 'Quiet Garden' on some days; see www.langstone-court.org.uk for details.

BERNITHAN COURT

Bernithan Court was built in the late 17th century (a barn has a datestone of 1695) but probably incorporates an earlier building, and has many architectural similarities with Langstone Court. For many years this was the seat of the Hoskyns family and it is said to have been visited by James I. It is noted as a fine example of a late 17th-century gentry house, possibly inspired by Troy House near Monmouth (built for the marquis of Worcester) or Castle House in Monmouth, both of which are typical post-Restoration houses. The interior retains a significant amount of its original fittings, including panelling and decorative plasterwork.

Once in this field, head up to the far right-hand corner, passing to the right of a Wellingtonia tree en route. Pass through the small gate here, then follow the line of the fence on your left in an arc round 'Way-go-through Cottage' to the track that services it on the far side. Turn right and head along this track. When it bends to the right in a sort of corner of the field and is about to drop downhill, cross the stile ahead of you and walk straight across the field, heading just to the right of the telegraph pole ahead of you, soon spotting a short length of track on the far side that leads from the field gateway to a road; aim for this. Keep an eye out for Bernithan Court on your left as you cross the field. Turn right once you reach the road, and this will lead you back to the church.

Walk 41
Garway Hill
& Kentchurch

6.25 miles, largely on the Herefordshire Trail, field edge paths, minor roads and tracks. Several stiles. Includes the site of an Iron Age farmstead, Second World War remains, castle sites and a possible visit to the grounds of Kentchurch Court.

Park near the letterbox and road junction with a signpost to Garway & Monmouth; to St Weonards and to Bagwylldiart, Pontrilas & Hereford (GR 447 249).

1 From the road junction, walk in the Hereford direction and turn left opposite the letterbox onto a gravelled track. Note the building on the right at the start of the track with a yellow 'Sun' sign on it.

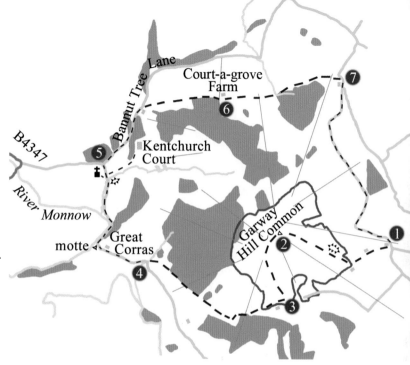

SUN SIGN
This building used to contain the Rising Sun alehouse, which operated between *circa* 1870 and 1920. It then became a post office and shop called The Sun (to which the sign relates) run by a number of people over the years and finally, in 1973, became a short-lived wholefood shop. Since then it has been a private dwelling.

Walk up the track to its end, where it passes through a gate onto Garway Hill Common. Turn right and walk up the fenceline on your right, following a major grassy track uphill towards the summit. Not far past where the fenceline on your right makes a 90 degree turn away from you, you come to a rough square of earthen banks on your right. This is the site of an Iron Age farmstead.

IRON AGE FARMSTEAD

A concentration of flint scrapers and waste flakes found on Garway Hill suggest that Neolithic people (4000-2000BC) made flint tools here. The flint must have been 'imported' as it is not found naturally in the area (the hill itself is formed of Old Red Sandstone rocks). In 2001 excavations at Little Garway Farm unearthed evidence of a Bronze Age Beaker burial, suggesting that the area was settled by then (though it may have been so earlier). Then, a few years later, aerial photography revealed a rectangular enclosure on a terrace on the south-west of the common; it was usually buried in bracken, though the more prominent enclosure alongside which the walk goes had long been known. Following countless theories as to what this enclosure might represent, in 2006, following a geophysical survey, three small exploratory trenches were dug. In one of these, in the fill of the surrounding ditch, several pieces of pottery were found dating to between 300 and 50BC (the Middle to Late Iron Age). In the centre of the site, evidence for a circular or oval structure was found, whilst at least part of the east-facing bank was faced in stone, unlike the other banks. Perhaps this was the side that the inhabitants most wanted to show off. Considering all the finds, the site is considered to have been a small farmstead, probably occupied by an extended family group consisting of up to 20 individuals at any one time, that was used from around 300BC possibly into the next millennium. Field boundaries stretch to the south of the site giving added weight to this theory.

SECOND WORLD WAR ROC POST

The octagonal brick-built structure is all that is left of a Second World War radio tracking station. Outside the foundations, at each corner, are concrete pads that supported the 'legs' of a timber tower that rose above the brick building. Other remains of the same date in the vicinity are of a barrack block enclosed within an embanked fire break, and the foundations of a building that housed the site's generator. Though the construction work was completed, the radio transmitters were never installed, and the wooden tower was dismantled in 1948.

Keep on up the grassy track to the summit of the hill, where you will find a red-brick octagonal structure, the remains of Second World War Royal Observer Corps post, and a trig point.

2 Turn left at this point on another wide grassy track which starts by heading towards the next hill to the west on the other side of the Monnow valley (the hill's name is Graig Syfyrddin). After 80 yards or so the path forks; take the left path, which soon bends to the left and gathers momentum down the hillside. Stay on this track, ignoring all options to right or left, the track itself staying above a slight bank on your right and passing just above the settlement of White Rocks in a form of cwm in the hillside on your left. The track eventually joins an earthen track at the edge of the common.

3 Turn right on the track and follow it along the hillside, passing above Little Castlefield Farm. Beyond the farm, keep following the fenceline on your left, slanting gently down and along the hillside. This will lead you to a gate which you go through, to enter what proves to be a large field. Keep following the fence on your left, though also staying to the right of a dip in the hillside, and keep shadowing the edge of the field to eventually head just to the right of its far left-hand corner, where you enter some woodland.

For the next part of the route, you will be keeping going in much the same direction, slanting along and gently down the hillside to eventually meet the road in the valley bottom.

Having entered the woodland, follow the path ahead which will lead you into a field. Once in the field, the path soon turns left downhill round a corner of fence and after about 50 yards then bears right along a grassy track that runs gently downhill through the field. When this track makes a sharp left turn to leave the field through a gateway, continue ahead towards the far bottom corner of the field, where you cross a stile. Follow the fenceline on your right and soon cross another stile into scrub woodland. Keep following the edge of the woodland on your right to another stile, and cross this into a field. Here, initially follow the field boundary with the wood on your right, but as this starts to bend to the right, keep on straight ahead across the field, aiming for a stile on the far side. Cross this, then a narrow field to a gate, and so enter the next field. Here the path bends slightly to the left, aiming for what looks like the far bottom corner of the field. As you approach it, you will find a gate that leads you out onto a minor road adjacent to a small stream, the field continuing on the far side of the stream.

④ Turn right on the road. In a few hundred yards Great Corras is on your right and earthworks in the orchard opposite. Just a bit further on, beyond a driveway off to the left and on a bend in the road, are the overgrown remains of Corras motte. Not far on again you can see an old ford across the river Monnow below to your left. Keep on the road and just before you come to the entrance driveway to Kentchurch Court (see overleaf), you will see an old moated site off to the right. A little further on, on the left, is Kentchurch church. Keep on along the road, turning right at the junction not far ahead; this is Bannut Tree Lane.

⑤ Keep on the road past some of the woods and gardens of Kentchurch Court on the right, till you reach Bannut Tree Farm, where you will leave the road.

Cross the second bridge on the right at the farm, and follow the track to the left of all the farm buildings to a gate into a field: the path heads up the hill, passing between the second and third of the telegraph poles that stand in the field. At this point the path bends right to follow a line of

GREAT CORRAS EARTHWORKS / MOTTE

Great Corras was where the Scudamore family (see under KENTCHURCH COURT overleaf) first settled and built a castle. The motte still rises to a height of 12 feet. A pill box was erected on it in the Second World War (since removed). The location of any baileys is disputed, but one may lie under the modern house whilst in 1988 what is believed to have been a bailey to the south of the motte was excavated and found to contain the foundations of a Norman chapel. This was enlarged sometime after 1200 and given a stone tower, but demolished around 1400, perhaps due to depopulation after the Black Death, with the stone being reused elsewhere.

The earthworks in the field opposite Great Corras probably represent the site of a deserted medieval village, which surveys indicate included a large rectangular building – probably either a barn or manor house, a building with possible foundations for a tower, a well and a pond.

KENTCHURCH MOATED SITE

To the right of the entrance drive to Kentchurch Court is a rectangular moated site with an entrance on the north-eastern side. The site may indicate the location of a castle in which the family lived in the 13th century or could be that of an ornamental feature or a folly.

KENTCHURCH COURT

Kentchurch has been in the Scudamore family for nearly 1,000 years. The first Scudamore recorded in the area was Ralph Scudamore in 1052, a stonemason brought over from Normandy by Edward the Confessor to build the castle in Ewyas Harold. A later branch of the Scudamores first settled at Great Corras before moving to Kentchurch Court in the 14th century, possibly via the moated site at the end of the present drive. Owain Glyndwr's daughter, Alice, married John Scudamore, and in Owain's later years, after his rising was over (see p.211) he is believed to have spent some time here, as well as at Monnington-on Wye and Croft Castle, where his other daughters had married into Herefordshire families. Sir James Scudamore, a jousting champion and courtier of Queen Elizabeth I, became the inspiration for Edmund Spenser's knight, Scudamour, in his epic poem *The Faerie Queene*.

In 1773, Anthony Keck redesigned the interior of the house. In 1795, John Nash remodelled the house in the Gothic style, work only completed under Thomas Tudor in the 1820s, though part of the early castle structure has been retained. Freak floods in 1959 caused severe damage, and it took two years for the house to dry out.

The house is open to the public on certain days in the year, and the gardens – which include a walled garden, vegetable garden, rhododendron wood and deer park – most weekdays, but to check go to http://kentchurchcourt.co.uk.

leads somewhat back on yourself and passes to the right of an old stone barn to reach a gate into the field ahead. Go through the gate, turn right and go through the next gate quickly reached on your right. Head diagonally across the field to the left-hand of two gates in this far corner. Through this head across the next, much wider, field to a gateway just below a stretch of woodland that clings to the hillside.

Once through this gate, keep to the edge of the woodland, now on your left, and you will presently join a track that leads you into and then through the woodland to reach a kissing gate on its far side. Through this, head across a short stretch of field to then go through another kissing gate. Once through this, follow the fence and hedgeline on your left in much the same direction, crossing two more field boundaries by gates to eventually emerge onto a track. Turn left on this to reach the minor road a few yards ahead.

❹ Cross the road and head up a few steps to a small gate into another field. Once in the field, head up the hillside, passing a line of trees and then following the field boundary on your right. (Look to your left for a good view of the columbarium.) Join the line of an old track that heads off half-left up and across the hillside to a gate at the top of the field, to the left of a set of new farm buildings. Go through this gate to emerge onto another minor road.

GARWAY COURT
There are several hypotheses for the origins of the name Garway, but one is that it derives from the Welsh *Gaergwy*, 'fort above the river'. To the south of Garway Court there is a spur where the land falls steeply on the west and less steeply to a tributary on the east. Some think that scarping here may indicate an early defensive site, though the scarping is more likely to be natural. A later castle site is thought to exist near the church, but this awaits excavation.

❺ Turn right on this, and follow it along between a set of new farm buildings. When you are adjacent to the entrance to the white-painted farmhouse (of Garway Court), turn left to pass between more farm buildings and enter a field. Follow the track across the field towards two gates in the far fenceline. Go through the right-hand one of these and then follow the fenceline on your left in a gentle curve up and along the hillside, passing above a narrow stretch of woodland and crossing through two more kissing gates at field boundaries as you approach a group of new houses. The path keeps to the left of these, leaving the final field by a gate to then follow a track to a road on which you turn right to return to your vehicle and the Moon.

your right into a field, which you head directly across. Cross the stile here and almost immediately another stile a few yards ahead, to then follow a field boundary on your left. Slightly to your right you will see Hardwicke church, designed by Thomas Tudor and built in 1849-51 after Clifford parish was divided in two. Cross a track ahead by a gate on one side and a stile on the other, and then pass out onto the B4348 just to the right of a small house.

7 Turn left on the B road, and immediately right onto a no-through road. Walk up this and when it divides, take the lane to the left which leads past Pen-y-lan Farm on your right and then becomes a track which you follow straight ahead to a gate that leads into a wood. Here you follow the bridleway marked by blue arrows, which bears right uphill. This becomes more of a path as it gently winds its way along and up the hillside. In due course it enters onto bracken-covered hillside, shortly after which it forks. Take the left-hand option, which takes you in an arc up the hillside to meet a track on which you turn right. Follow the track to meet a road.

8 Turn right on this and walk along it through woodland till you get to a T-junction. Turn right here, the road dropping downhill. Shortly after making a short, steep descent, the road swings right and then sharply left. At this left bend, take a track off to the right which passes between field boundaries and soon curves gently to the right to emerge near a house. Bear left on the lane

and once you've passed an old barn on your left and a second house on the right, and are just about to leave the 'farmyard', pass through a gate on your left into a field (yellow waymarking signs may be hard to discern here).

9 Cross this field staying parallel to the field boundary on your left to join a track on the far side of the field. Turn left on the track and cross the stream by a footbridge to the left of the old mill, just before the cattle grid, and head up the bank on the far side to stand on the edge of a large field. The line of the path may not be obvious here, but look across to the far side of the field and you should see a couple of trees which mark the line of a hedgerow just over the brow of the slope. You want to aim for the point where this hedgerow meets the wood at its right-hand end. (Once again avoid heading for a stile you may be able to spot in the fence off to your right; this area is criss-crossed with paths!)

As you walk across the field you will eventually spot a gateway into the next field at the hedgerow/woodland junction. Once in the next field, cross it on much the same line, aiming for a marker post (hopefully still standing). Here you will find a crossing point into the next, smaller, field, which you cross to the top left-hand corner, heading for a stile. Once over this stile, turn right and follow the hedge, to reach another plank bridge and stile. Over these, cross some open ground, aiming to the left of a cottage, to then follow the edge of some woodland to your right. You pass through one field boundary before eventually reaching the B4348.

⑩ Cross the B road and turn right on it, to immediately cross over the stile into the field now on your left. The line of the path may not be clear at this point, but aim a little to the right of the right-hand one of the two telegraph poles you can see towards the middle far side of the field, and cross the field on this roughly diagonal line. As you cross you will eventually see a footpath gate on the far side which you go through, followed by a bridge across the stream beyond. Go up the bank on the far side, then turn left somewhat to shadow the line of the stream you've just crossed, and go through the footpath gate that is adjacent to a field gate and which you should soon see in the fence ahead. Once through the gate, you'll see that a corner of a field to the left juts into the field you're in. Your path crosses the field you're in, passing about 20 yards to the right of this corner.

As you cross the field you will see the entrance to a 'passage' through the hedgerow. Once through this, head across the next field to its top far corner where it meets the woodland, then cross the stile and follow the edge of the woodland, keeping it on your right (you can see Priory Farm below to the left). When you reach a rendered

CLIFFORD PRIORY

Clifford Priory was founded as daughter house of the Cluniac priory of Lewes in Sussex around 1130 by the first Walter de Clifford's brother, Simon fitz Richard. The priory itself has long since vanished, being largely incorporated after the Dissolution into the building that is now Priory Farm. Leland noted in 1535 that the priory was the burial place of the Cliffords, 'but all destroyed'. Near the farm buildings are the remains of old fishponds.

1930s-style house you cross one stile to its immediate right, follow the field boundary on your left, and cross another stile to emerge in another field. Cross the stone track and look across the field, where you should be able to see the tower of Clifford church. You want to aim to the right of this, and heading across this field on that line you should soon see a stile ahead of you. Cross this and then cut across the left-hand corner of the next field to where you judge is the near corner of the churchyard, and here you will find a gate into the churchyard.

⓫ Cross the churchyard on the diagonal you're on, passing the entrance to the church, and emerge onto a road junction. Diagonally cross this to the path which makes a 'cross-roads' of the junction, heading up the bank and then following a stone wall on your left. You soon enter a small field, which you cross diagonally to the far corner. Cross over the stile here into the next field and turn right to almost immediately cross over another stile into some woodland. The path goes a few yards into the wood, then turns left and shadows the edge of the wood some 20 yards away to eventually emerge into another field. This you cross to a stile towards the far right-hand corner, this stile leading to a path back across the railway line. Once over this and in the field beyond, hopefully you'll recognize it as the first field of your walk! Walk down the field boundary on your left to cross back over the stile by which you first entered the field, and down the path back to the road on which you parked.

EFFIGY IN CLIFFORD CHURCH
The effigy in the recess on the north side of the chancel is one of the earliest in the country – it may date from the late 1200s – and one of only a hundred or so medieval wooden effigies left in Britain. Its subject is a priest in Eucharistic vestments, and the figure may originally have been brightly painted, but only tiny remnants of colour remain. The effigy is said to commemorate a monk who died defending the priory's food stocks from marauders.

Walk 44
Dorstone, Arthur's Stone & Merbach Hill

5.75 miles, largely on paths across pasture, field edge paths, tracks and minor roads. Several stiles. Includes a castle site, old quarries, a squatter village, Arthur's Stone and an old inn.

Park near the Pandy Inn (GR 314 416). Looking at the inn, the site of Dorstone Castle is to the right.

1 With your back to the inn, walk left along the road for a few yards, then turn down the right-hand side of the triangular 'green'. Go straight on to cross a lane, cross a bridge over a stream, and pick up the track and path that leads round the left-hand side of the churchyard.

Cross the B road and carry on on the footpath that initially follows the fenceline to the right of the recreation ground, and then slants across a corner of it to reach a footbridge across the headwaters of the river Dore. Cross the line of the old Golden Valley Railway (see p.305),

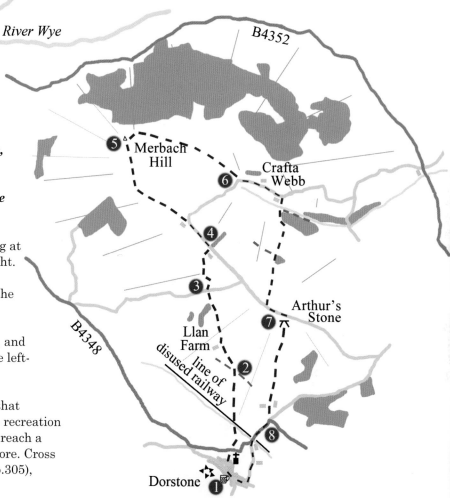

DORSTONE CHURCH AND PANDY INN

A chapel at the church is said to have been founded by Richard de Brito, one of the murderers of St Thomas à Becket, or by one of his descendants. Brito is said to have broken his sword during the execution: 'But the third knight [Brito] inflicted a grave wound on the fallen one; with this blow he shattered the sword on the stone and his crown, which was large, separated from his head so that the blood turned white from the brain yet no less did the brain turn red from the blood; it purpled the appearance of the church with the colors of the lily and the rose, the colors of the Virgin and Mother and the life and death of the confessor and martyr.' One story has it that de Brito fled to Dorstone and built a chapel to expiate his sins, but it is more likely that the four knights fled to Scotland and thence Knaresborough Castle, were excommunicated by the pope and ordered to undertake penitentiary pilgrimages to the Holy Land for a period of 14 years, and that the chapel was built around 1256 by members of de Brito's family. Why they should have come to this corner of Herefordshire is puzzling. Descended from a Somerset family, the name is a version of 'le Breton', which might explain why de Brito spent his last days in Jersey, where he is believed to have died. In any event, the medieval church at Dorstone was demolished in 1827, and the shoddily built replacement was also knocked down and the current church erected; it incorporates a few medieval features that survived the two rebuilds. The Pandy Inn is said to date from 1185, and also to have been built by Richard de Brito.

and go through the gate into a field. Diagonally cross this field to a gate in the far left-hand corner – or turn left and follow the edge of the field if it's obstructed by crops.

2 Go through the gate and cross a sunken path to climb the steps to a gate into the field opposite; cross to the far left corner of the field. Turn left along a tarmacked lane and walk towards the farm buildings ahead. The path has recently been diverted here from the course shown on OS maps. About 100 yards *before* you reach the farm, cross a stile on the right. Head diagonally across the field, aiming to the right of the farm buildings to reach another stile. Cross this and cross the next field, keeping just to the right

DORSTONE CASTLE

The oval-shaped motte rises some 9m above the bottom of the surrounding ditch, and a recent geophysical survey suggests that it once supported a shell keep, with a D-shaped tower flanking the entrance. Presumably much of the stone from this supplied the building material for the nearby houses. A kidney-shaped bailey lies between the road and the motte in which further traces of buried stone have been found, whilst loose stone includes voussoirs and dressed tufa. The castle may be the site referred to as Dodintune in the Domesday Survey, and if so was then held by Drogi, son of Poyntz. From the late 12th to the early 14th century it was held by the de Solers family. In 1403 it was ordered that it be put into repair against Owain Glyndwr, but as nothing is heard of it thereafter it may have suffered at his hands.

of the farm buildings. Leave the field in the far corner over a stile opposite a cattle shed. Turn right on the track and follow it uphill. Pass through a narrow band of woodland, cross a stream and go through a gate, and then your path diverges from the track; you bear right to head for a stile on the far side of a field. Cross this stile to find yourself on a minor road.

3 Turn left on the road and almost immediately on your right you'll see a stile into another field. Enter this field and head up the hillside, following the field boundary on your right. Leave the field at the far side to find yourself on a track, on which you turn left. After some tens of yards and immediately past the next field boundary that heads away uphill to your right, go over a stile on the

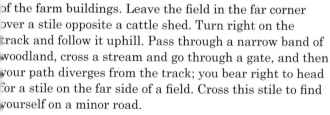

MERBACH HILL

The quarry near the trig point, a source of both sandstone and limestone, might originally have supplied the stone for the construction of Arthur's Stone (see p.316), but more recently was a source of limestone for three lime-kilns on the lower slopes of the hill. The resultant lime was mainly used for lowering the acidity of the clay soil that covers most of Herefordshire to improve growing conditions for crops, but would have also have been used for mortar and for lime-washing the walls of houses. It would also have been useful as a bleach in paper-making, and to line cess pits to help kill germs and suppress noxious smells.

right, and walk uphill, slightly diverging from the field boundary on your right to cross into the next field. Once in this field, follow the field boundary on your right to reach the minor road at the far side.

4 Turn left on this and walk along to where it makes a 90 degree turn to the right. At this point, go straight ahead through the gate and walk along the hillside. Almost immediately, the track takes a 90 degree left-hand bend. Keep going straight ahead, following the lines

---

CRAFTA WEBB

In Victorian times, this part of Bredwardine Hill was home to Crafta Webb, a settlement where many poor families lived. People may have settled here hoping to receive assistance through the Jarvis Charity. George Jarvis was a local resident who made a fortune elsewhere and returned to provide charity to the villagers of Bredwardine, Letton and Staunton-on-Wye. (For more on the Jarvis Charity see p.214.) An archaeological project in 2007 revealed that the settlement consisted of ten cottages/workshops built of local sandstone, nine of them measuring about 7m by 4m, just one storey high, and the tenth a larger building that may have had two storeys. Some stonework remains. It seems that the inhabitants didn't just rely on charity, if that was their reason for settling here, but that they worked the seam of limestone that runs through the hill, quarrying the stone and perhaps operating a limekiln that remains to the south-east.

---

of old field boundaries on your left and keeping roughly to the contour of the hillside, which curves initially to the left, and then to the right. After about half a mile you'll come to a gate that leads to the bracken-covered summit of Merbach Hill. Go ahead and make for the trig point.

5 Facing the view down into the Wye Valley from the trig point, turn right and take the lower of the two paths, the one closest to the drop down the hillside. At a crossroads of paths, go straight ahead to join the Wye Valley Walk. At another crossroads of paths, the Wye Valley Walk goes straight ahead; you leave it at this point to turn right. Carry on along this path until you meet another track, where you turn left and go through a gate onto a track (which may be overgrown) which leads straight on till you reach a minor road.

6 Turn left on this (effectively carrying on straight ahead) and walk downhill, passing through the settlement of Crafta Webb, till the road makes a sharp bend to the left. Here, turn right onto a short piece of track which passes a house to the right. Ignore the footpath sign off to the left, and once in the field at the end of this short track, turn half-left and follow the old routeway up to the corner of woodland, and then initially follow the woodland on your left. Adjacent to a gate into the woodland, the path continues on the line on which you've been walking (in other words diverges slightly from the woodland) to reach the hedgeline above you. Cross this by a stile just

315

ARTHUR'S STONE

This Neolithic long barrow dates from between 3400 and 2400 BC and is one of the most northerly tombs of the style known as Severn-Cotswold, of which 200 dating from the middle to late Neolithic were built across the south-west Midlands and central Wales. Nine upright stones support an enormous capstone believed to weigh some 25 tonnes over the area that would have contained the burials, and there is also an entrance passage with an unorthodox right-angled bend and a stone that partially blocks the passage. The whole would have been covered by an earthen mound that would have spread across the line of the present road. It has been calculated that the tomb would have taken between 7,000 and 16,000 man hours to build (or between 875 and 2,000 eight-hour days), the labour probably coming from a Neolithic settlement that has been discovered further south on the ridge which may have been home to some 250 people. The tomb has never been excavated, though it has clearly been robbed of much material over the years, but similar examples have been found to contain incomplete skeletal remains of several bodies, together with flint flakes, arrowheads and pottery. It is thought that bodies may have been submitted to a process of excarnation – left in the open for wild beasts and birds to clean the bones, which were then gathered and placed in the tombs, during which process some bones almost certainly went missing or were carried off by the beasts and birds, explaining why the skeletal remains are invariably incomplete.

As with many Neolithic tombs, the monument is not right on the crest of a hill, probably being sited so that it was more easily seen from the valley bottom and so helping delineate and mark out a home territory. It has been suggested that the reason for the right-angled bend is so that each of the arms of the tomb points to one end of the line of the Black Mountains, perhaps again to give a sense of 'territory'. The tomb probably acted as a site for ritual activity as well, and the isolated stone on the south-western side may have formed part of a false entrance that also gave a visual focus for ceremonies.

Its name has been acquired due to folklore, one belief being that it had once contained the body of King Arthur, another that here Arthur fought a giant which he killed and buried in the tomb.

to the right of a field gate, and then follow the field boundary on your right to reach a stile in the far right-hand corner of this next field. Once over the stile, turn slightly left away from the field boundary on your right and make for a gate on the far side of the field, passing a scattered group of larches on your left and then a boggy hollow on your right. Once through the gate, follow the field boundary on your left to reach a minor road. Turn left on this and you will quickly come to Arthur's Stone on the right-hand side.

7 Take the footpath just below Arthur's Stone, heading almost directly downhill, and then turning gently to the left and through a gate to pick up a track that leads above a pond to your left and so angles downhill, passing through a few gates, to eventually keep to the left of the farmhouse near the bottom of the slope and so emerge at a crossroads of minor roads.

8 Head over this crossroads on the B4348 and downhill to once again cross the river Dore, then turn left on the bend to take the minor road back into the village, ignoring the first turning to the right, to turn right at the T-junction a short distance beyond to return to the Pandy Inn.

Walk 45
Cusop

3.75 miles, largely on paths across pastureland, through woodland or along field edges, as well as minor roads and tracks. Several stiles. Includes a church, valley industry and a castle site.

Park in the car park by the church in Cusop (GR 239 415). As the map shows, you could choose to combine this walk with Walk 46.

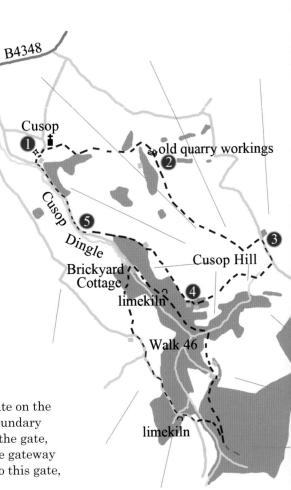

CUSOP CHURCH
Under the large yew tree by the south-east corner of the church lies the grave of William Seward, a follower of Wesley and Whitfield who in 1740 was injured by a mob when preaching in Hay and died a week after the incident.

The church itself is Norman, but was much restored in 1857.

❶ Walk through the churchyard to the right of the church to the gate on the far side and pass out into the field. Turn right and follow the field boundary on your right to the gate in the corner of the field. Cross the stile by the gate, then follow the field boundary and stream on your right, round to the gateway near the top right-hand corner of the field. Once over the stile next to this gate,

LIMEKILNS

Lime production was carried out up the Dulas valley, exploiting a narrow bed of limestone, in the later 18th and earlier 19th centuries, the remains of the kilns encountered on this walk being particularly impressive. Local historian Theophilus Jones at the beginning of the 19th century noted that because of the distance from the coal-pits the expense of producing lime locally was very great. Unsurprisingly the industry declined during the later 19th century due to competition from larger producers elsewhere, especially following the construction of the Hay to Brecon tramroad in the early 19th century.

To extract the lime, a coal fire was lit at the base of the shaft. Alternating layers of coal and limestone pieces (ideally between 1 and 2½ inches in size) were then tipped into the 'charge hole' at the top. Once the fire was lit and the fuel in the charge hole started to burn, there was no need for the bottom fire. The arched opening, known as the 'kiln eye', allowed air to feed the mix, which would keep slowly burning day after day with temperatures reaching over 900 degrees C. As the resultant powdery mixture – quicklime – dropped through the grate into the 'draw hole' it was raked out and bagged. Further layers of coal and limestone were added at the top to allow continuous burning.

and when this drops away down the slope, the path continues across the hillside, rising slightly up it to pass through a line of mature trees. Beyond these trees you aim for the far top corner of the field, near where another stream tumbles down a deeply cut bed towards the Dulas Brook.

2 Cross the stile here, and turn right to follow the path along the fence and then above the house, and then along a fence again. Further on you cross the fence to follow it on your left for a brief distance, before crossing back over again. The path will widen out to a grassy strip, passing a tree that may be festooned with Christmas decorations (at least it has been each time we've walked this path) and later still dropping down to join a wide track. Turn sharp right on this and follow it down to a gate. Once through the gate, keep left on the lane you join, ford the shallow stream and follow the lane uphill and round to the left to join a road.

3 Turn right, soon passing another limekiln on your left. Eventually, the road you're on will join the one from Hay up into the Black Mountains and Capel-y-ffin. Here, turn right (in effect continuing straight ahead) in the direction of Hay, but when the road presently bends to the left by a farmhouse, go right onto the grassy triangle and then through the field gate in the far corner. Once in the field, follow the hedgeline and stream on your left across and then more directly down the hillside, crossing field boundaries as you come to them. This will lead you to a footbridge near Brickyard Cottage and so to your vehicle.

Walk 47
Craswall

3.25 miles, on tracks, field edge paths (usually across pasture) and minor roads. A few stiles. Includes a church and the remains of a priory. In wet weather Wellingtons may be the best choice of footwear!

Park on the lane by the Bulls Head Inn (GR 278 360). (For the inn's opening hours, check www. bullsheadcraswall.co.uk.)

❶ With your back to the entrance pathway to the pub, turn right on the road and so round the corner and downhill to cross a stream and then continue up the road on the far side. Where the road bends to the left, you may wish to visit the church.

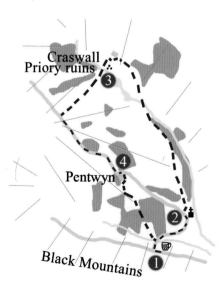

CRASWALL CHURCH

The church is notable for its simplicity and setting. It probably dates from the 13th century, with some Perpendicular windows and an east window that is supposed to have come from the nearby priory. There is, unusually, stone seating along the outside of the east and south walls of the church, as well as remnants of it round the yew in the south-east corner of the churchyard. The shallow depression adjoining the north wall of the church marks the site of a fives court; the stone tablets fixed to the wall may have been for recording the score. The depression in the north-west corner of the churchyard is believed to have been a cockpit for staging cock fights.

2 The walk itself takes the short length of track off to the right just past the churchyard and then almost immediately forks left over a cattle grid and into a field. Follow the track which contours the hillside and passes some farm buildings to their left, then crossing a small stream. Cross the next field on the same line to a gate on the opposite side. Cross the stream here and then go through the left-hand gate to then follow the field boundary on your right. At the far end of the field ignore a path that crosses yours at right angles and keep ahead to cross another stream and go through a gate into the next field. Keep on roughly the same line across this field to the left of a group of larch trees where the path passes through a field gate to join a track.

Walk along this track, which keeps to the edge of the woodland, and leave it by another field gate. The path crosses the field you're now in on much the same line as you've been walking, crossing by a footpath gate into the field beyond. At this point the path heads across the bottom of this field to a field gate. Through this gate, cross one stream and walk along a path to the left of another to a further footpath gate. Cross the stream immediately beyond this gate and walk along the path-cum-track into the bottom corner of a field.

Once in this field, the path heads diagonally up and across the field to the far top corner (if you look half-left at this point you can see the priory's fishpond in the valley bottom and to its right the remains of the priory buildings). Here it passes through a field gate and then follows the field boundary

CRASWALL PRIORY

Craswall Priory was founded as a house of the Grandmontine Order c.1225 by Walter de Lacy. The founder of this order was Stephen of Thiers, who had been so impressed by the lives of the hermits he had seen in Calabria that he decided to form his own hermitage and lived a life of solitude in the valley of Muret, near Limoges. Stephen left no written 'rule', but his maxim was 'There is no rule save the Gospel of Christ' and he believed in an austere life of prayer, as would befit a hermit. Disciples gathered close by, and after Stephen's death, Etienne de Luciac established the Order, which grew to a total of 60 houses, mainly in Normandy, Anjou and Aquitaine, and three in England: Alberbury (Shropshire), Grosmont (just over the border in Monmouthshire) and Craswall. These English priories survived the suppression of many alien monasteries (those whose mother house was overseas) and continued in existence until 1462. Craswall was visited by Henry III in 1233.

The church consisted of a nave with a semicircular apsidal eastern end, of which walls remain to a considerable height in places. A cloister lay to the south; there are traces of foundations for the arcade wall. To the east of the cloister lay (from north to south) a small sacristy which would have been roofed with a barrel vault, a passage and the chapter house of which some of the walling remains up to windowsill level, together with the bases of two circular columns in the middle of the room which would have divided it into six vaulted bays. The western range of buildings and frater to the south of the cloister have been partially eroded by the stream which seems to have been diverted since the priory's suppression. To the east of the frater and south of the chapter house lay the warming house, with the monks' dormitory to its east. There are remnants of other buildings, and of the wall enclosing the site.

To the south-east of the priory, at the confluence of two streams, there is an impressive dam some 2.5m high that retains what was the monastery's fishpond. A more recent dam and pond lie upstream of this.

328

on your right to another field gate which leads into a farmyard. Keep on the track past a farm building on your right, to turn left when facing a large group of buildings and walk down the lane that serves the farm. This will curve you round and down to the valley bottom, where you can visit the remains of Craswall Priory on your left.

3 Continue up the lane to the road junction, where you turn left. Follow the road along till you come to a farm (Pentwyn) on your right.

4 Immediately to the right of the Nissen hut 'garage', go through the gateway into the farmyard which you leave by another gateway into the field beyond. The path now parallels the line of buildings and then the field boundary on your right but stays a few yards out into the field, heading towards the bottom right-hand corner of the field. Here you cross into the field below by a stile. The path then turns to all but diagonally cross this field towards the bottom left-hand corner, where a stile leads you into the next field below. Follow the stream on your left and half-way down the field cross the stream then turn downhill on a path through the woodland to reach a stile into another field. The path then swings slightly left to the bottom left-hand corner of this field, crossing a stream and line of trees en route, where a footbridge will lead you out onto a road. Turn right on this to return to the inn and your vehicle.

your left, and when this turns left, keep on ahead across the field, aiming about 100 yards to the left of the field gate on the far side. As you approach the far side, you should see a stile in the hedge; cross this, and turn left on the road. Here you have an amazing 360 degree view (at least, if you are tall enough to see over the hedges!)

❸ After a few yards along the road, turn right onto a track marked as the entrance to 'Pentwyn'. Keep on this track (passing a turn to the right to Pentwyn) and enter a farmyard. Keep on the track, leaving all the farm buildings to your left and the farmhouse to your right, heading down to a gate to the right of a small stone barn. Go through this gate, the path then first leading right to the banks of a small brook, then turning left (without crossing the brook) to head to a point roughly half-way along the hedge on the far side of the field where there is a stile and footbridge. Cross these and take the path which stays initially to the left of a line of trees across the field, then turns right through them to descend into the farmyard of Lower House Farm.

❹ Walk through this and join the track that serves the farmyard. Almost immediately after you've left the farmyard, with the track stretching straight ahead of you, turn left through a gate into a field. Diagonally cross this field, keeping immediately to the right of a hollow and a line of trees. This will lead to a series of stiles, with the path perched immediately above the Escley Brook. The third stile will lead you back into a field, where you turn right and follow the fence down to a gate and footbridge which you cross, then turn left to go through a gate between two fields. The path then passes just to the left of an old stone building that stands close by, where it goes through a gate, and then follows the field boundary on your left up to a point where it again meets the lane that serves Lower House Farm. Here it passes through a gate onto a road.

❺ Turn right on the road and follow it for about half a mile, when you should notice the entranceway to The Quakers on your left. About 180 yards after this, on the right, is a field gate into the Christopher Cadbury Nature Reserve. Just inside the field entrance, slightly hidden behind the hedge, is a board which tells you something about the reserve (which the walk will be crossing shortly). Continue along the road for about 100 yards, then go through the footpath gate on the right and take the path into the far end of the nature reserve.

❻ Follow the field boundary on your left, passing a stone-built cottage to a bridge across the Escley Brook. Over the bridge, the footpath is in a bit of a state. Whilst there are marker posts buried in the woodland, this is covered in brambles and various obstacles, so it is best to turn right and cross a small brook reached after about 20 yards, then turn uphill to walk through a glade, keeping to the edge of the brook that you've just crossed and its abutting

CHRISTOPHER CADBURY NATURE RESERVE
This ancient meadow is believed never to have been treated with artificial fertilizers or herbicide. The hillside is contoured by two old leats, presumably used to irrigate the field to encourage early grass growth. The meadow is believed to support 160 species of flora.

vegetation. As you near the top of the glade, you'll see the line of a sunken track that leads slightly to the right. Follow the line of this to a corner of the wood, where you'll find a gate out into the field above. Go through this gate and follow the field boundary on your right to near the far end of the field and go through a field gate out onto a track near a stone building.

7 Turn right on the track and walk past Glibes Farm, the track becoming a road and in a few hundred yards passing Wern Derris standing stone on your right, in a corner of a field just beyond the field alongside the road. There is a track that leads to the stone, but bear in mind that it stands on private ground. Keep on the lane down to a crossroads, which you go straight over and so down to another road junction. Turn left and then right on the road to return to your vehicle.

Walk 49
St Margarets

4.25 miles, largely on paths across fields and along field edges (usually over pastureland), woodland tracks, and minor roads. A few stiles. Includes two churches with the option to visit a third nearby.

Park near the church at Turnastone (GR 357 365).

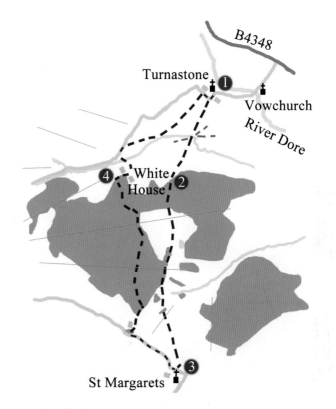

❶ With your back to the churchyard entrance, turn right and walk down the road past the old garage, and at the bend just past the garage, turn left past Brook Cottage onto a track which leads to a gate into a field. In the field, turn slightly right and head just to the right of a new bridge for farm vehicles at the far side of the field. A number of footpaths meet here. To find the correct one, take the grassy crossing (through a field gate) over the stream, between the farm bridge on your left and the footbridge on your right (or just take the farm bridge if the grassy crossing is overgrown). Cross the field you enter to its far top corner just below the woodland.

❷ Pass into the woodland, almost immediately crossing a fenceline, and then follow the well waymarked path that winds its way up the hillside and leaves the wood at the top by a gate. The path then turns left to follow the edge of the wood on your left and thence a series of field boundaries which curve gently to the right. After crossing a field boundary, follow the left-hand edge of a large field. At the top of the field, go through a gate to enter a wood. Follow the path which keeps to its left-hand edge, shortly to emerge into another field.

VOWCHURCH AND TURNASTONE CHURCHES

These are two small Norman churches (both with some subsequent rebuilding and adaptation) separated by some 500 yards. The church at Turnastone has a wagon roof, and an incised alabaster slab to Thomas ap Harry and his wife who died in 1522. That at Vowchurch is unusual for having a timber structure separate from the walls to support the roof; indeed the walls were built later. The screen bears a date of 1613, and its rough carvings include figures either side of the doorway taken to represent Adam and Eve, though pears, not apples, have been carved above their heads.

At this point, turn slightly right, heading to a point about 50 yards left of a small thicket of firs on the other side of the field, and downhill to cross a stream below the thicket. Once over the stream the path crosses a stile, then heads left to cross another stile just to the right of a stunted oak tree and pass through a small coppice. Once through this and over another stile, the path continues on much the same line. Head for the open ridge between the trees, and then make for the top left corner of the large field. Here you will find a stile that leads you out onto a wide green lane. Follow this and it will lead you into a small field. Head for the far right-hand corner and this will lead you onto a short track and so through a gate and down to a minor road. Turn left on this to reach St Margarets church.

ST MARGARETS CHURCH

This simple church in its isolated and windswept setting is notable for its rood screen and its east window. (The glass dates from the 20th century and depicts St Margaret as a shepherdess.) The screen is of pale oak, has a head beam (that against the chancel wall) carved with an oak trail and top and drop cresting, whilst the loft coving has been divided into 42 square panels at the intersections of which are 30 carved bosses, 21 of which are original. The bressumer (on which the front of the loft coving rests) is carved with two trails, one of vine and the other of serrated leaves. Again there is top and drop cresting. The front of the parapet would have originally contained ornamentation, probably figures, and there is evidence that the panels would have been painted. The top beam, above the panels, is unusually carved with a trail of hawthorn, again with top and drop cresting (much of it renewed). The bressumer is supported by two richly carved posts, which bear niches that probably once carried statuettes. It has been described as 'one of the most satisfying examples of late medieval screenwork to survive anywhere in England or Wales', its construction techniques indicating it was carved by a Welsh school of carvers.

3 After leaving the churchyard, turn left on the road and follow this along the ridge, with its views to the Black Mountains on the left, until you reach Shobdon Farm on the right. Here, pass the farm drive and after a few yards take a footpath off to the right, over a stile into a small coppice. The potentially overgrown path through the coppice leads back to the farm drive, and if too overgrown for ease of walking, you may wish just to head straight down the farm drive. In either event, walk on along the drive past the farmhouse, pass through a gate and continue along the track down towards some farm buildings. Just before you reach them, bear slightly right to pass through a field gate and follow the track along the edge of a long field. Further on it enters some woodland near a small barn, after which it starts to take a more determined course down the hill, bending left and then

THE WHITE HOUSE

The first known owner of the White House was a Symond Parry in 1545, who is thought to have acquired it from the Church at the time of the Dissolution. He was the brother of Blanche Parry, who was a 'gentlewoman of Elizabeth I's privy chamber'. In the late 1500s the house passed via marriage to Rowland Vaughan, a soldier in the Irish wars who was named as the captain of 100 men at the time of the Armada, but who is best known locally for his book *Most approved and long experienced water works* .... Published in 1610, this explained an elaborate system of irrigation that he constructed along the Golden Valley from Peterchurch, but lacked crucial details. The aim was to distribute over the low-lying pastures the silt that is washed down the hillsides in the many streams. His main 'trench-royalle' can largely be traced south from Peterchurch, but many of the waterways that led from the redirected streams have since disappeared, infilled to allow modern machinery to work the fields and mow the grass.

In the 1700s the estate was the subject of many legal squabbles over rights of inheritance, and by the 1800s the house was in great need of repair. At one time it was going to be knocked down, but in the event just the north and east ends were rebuilt in the early 1800s with stone and timber from the estate, the white-painted parts indicating the surviving portions of the original Tudor house. In 1813 over 3,000 oaks from the woods were sold to be taken down the Wye and used for building ships for the Royal Navy, the money raised paying for the rebuilding of the house.

right near some buildings. Not far after this bend you pass some earthworks on your right, likely to mask the remains of some limekilns or an old quarry, or be part of landscaping carried out when the White House (the Tudor mansion you will shortly be coming to) was restored in the early 1800s. Keep on the track, which near the bottom of the wood passes the entrance to White House.

4 Keep following what is now a tarmacked lane down to the road, on which you turn right. You can follow this road back to your vehicle or, after a few yards, cross the stile on your right and head across to the far right-hand

corner of the field, the last stretch being alongside a small stream. Once across the field boundary here, shadow the hedge-line on the right. (The path adopts straight lines, unlike the curving line of the hedge.) At the road at the end of the field, pass back out over a stile next to a large gate and turn right on the road to return to your vehicle.

346

immediately take a track off to the left. After about 150 yards you will reach the unfenced hillside of the Black Mountains on your right. Cross a brook as you reach this unfenced area, and immediately take the path that slants up the hillside. This quickly turns to the right to cross back over the brook slightly below a green 'hut' which houses a pump and water tank. Ahead of you, you should see the line of the path you want to follow, slanting up the flank of the hillside; it may be easier to do so when the bracken is not flourishing. Take this path (a continuation of where you crossed the brook). You soon cross two paths, but need to keep going till you reach a third path (ignoring all sheep trails), reached about 100 yards after passing just below a single stunted tree. Turn left on this third path and follow it up onto the ridge, continuing across the ridge till you meet a wide track. This is the Offa's Dyke Path, which runs along the top of the ridge.

4 Turn left on the path and follow it past a trig point and downhill onto a narrow neck of the ridge. Here you will find a small 'gravestone' type marker, indicating (if you can make out the letters) that Llanthony is reached along a path to the right (shown in the photograph opposite), and Longtown along one to the left.

5 It is the left-hand one you take, a comfortably wide grassy track that slants on a fairly constant gradient down across the hillside. In due course it follows a field boundary and then meets a track which roughly follows the contour of the hillside. Turn left on this track and follow the field boundary

PONTHENDRE

A large circular motte stands some 10m above a surrounding ditch, with a crescent-shaped bailey on the north-east. Excavations in 2016 and 2017 showed that the castle was never completed, and the suggestion is that it was being constructed to impede the Welsh who held Longtown, the de Lacys not having sufficient manpower shortly after the Conquest to manage the task of taking the fort enhanced under Harold Godwinson. It was probably with the attack by William fitz Osbern, earl of Hereford, and the de Lacys on Brycheiniog shortly after construction of the castle began that the Welsh were cleared from Longtown, where the de Lacys then concentrated their castle building (see LONGTOWN CASTLE above).

river Monnow, crossing stone stiles into and out of the churchyard, and then passing through gates and over stiles as it first shadows the river, then a hedge on your right delineating a small field above the river and then a holloway across another small field. After you've crossed a large stone stile, the path follows the field boundary on your left to a pair of stone stiles that help you cross an ancient trackway that leads to the river, where you rejoin the road. Here turn right, noticing Ponthendre on your left as you cross the bridge, and keep on the 'main' road back to your vehicle.

❷ Head across the field keeping to the left of the tree-clad motte, alongside which you join a concrete track. This leads you to a gate into a yard that contains a small dilapidated farm building. Enter the yard and keep to the left of the building to follow the hard standing to another gate. Go through this gate into a field and walk along the hedge on your left, on the other side of which is a sharp drop into a small side valley. When you come to two metal gates on the left, go through the left-hand footpath gate into another field and walk along the hedgeline on your right. Go through the gate ahead into the next field and continue walking along the hedgeline, (ignoring a stile you reach on your right), to reach another gate in the top right-hand corner of the field. Go through this gate and follow the hedgeline now on your left to the top left-hand corner of this next field. Once through the footpath gate here, head across a corner of this field to its far right-hand corner where a stile can be found. Cross this and wend your way between a steep drop down to woods on the right and an old quarry on your left, passing between the trunks of the trees.

Once the other side of the quarry and in a field, the line of the path diverges from the line of the wood and slants across the rise to aim for (once it comes into view) a corner of another field that juts into this one. Walk around the outer edge of this corner, and then follow the hedgeline on your right gently downhill, passing through a gateway then past the remains of a farm building, through another two gateways and then through a further gate to the left of a farmhouse into the farmyard of Wigga farm.

3 Walk through the farmyard, in which you bear right to pass through a small gate immediately to the left of the side wall of the farmhouse. Follow the track along the fence on your right to a stile adjacent to a gate into the next field. Once over the stile you want to head for the far right-hand corner of the field you've entered, where you will find a stile into some woodland, the stile initially screened by a line of trees that are in the field itself. Over this stile, cross the stream and follow it downhill to a second stile, and thence continue a short distance to a third stile which will lead you into a field. Follow the edge of the wood on your right downhill, then when you reach a sunken hollow that leads directly downhill, follow this down to the stream on your left, bearing right here to walk to a gate out onto a road.

4 Turn right on the road and walk past Dulas parish church (now closed), shortly after which you turn left onto the drive to Dulas Court care home. Walk along the drive through the gardens of the court, the path staying

DULAS CHURCH AND COURT

The original Norman church was built *circa* 1200 in the valley below the site of the current church. This was demolished when the new church was built in 1865 to the design of G.C. Haddon, one arch of the old church being moved and reused as an entrance to a garden north of Dulas Court. The base of an old cross still remains near the site of the old church. The present Dulas Court was built shortly after 1858. In 1968 Mary Abbott gave the house and grounds to the Trustees of the Musicians' Benevolent Fund, and they developed it into a home for retired musicians, commemorations of some of whom can be seen in the line of gravestones alongside the path to the church. There is an information board in the churchyard about the management of the site for the benefit of wildlife.

on the drive to the far end of the court, then bearing right through the visitors' car park and over a bridge across the Dulas brook. Once over this bridge and before you reach a house on the right, turn right on a footpath that heads across a grassy patch and passes below the remnants of a walled garden, shortly crossing a stile into a field. Once in this field head uphill to a stile in its top corner. Cross this stile into the wood and immediately turn right on a grassy track. Turn right again at a crossroads of tracks soon reached. Turn right at the next fork and then almost immediately left onto a smaller path. The path at these last two junctions and then through the woodland is well waymarked. The path heads up the hillside to leave the woodland by a stile.

In the field beyond this stile, follow the line of large single trees up the hillside, and where these meet a hedgerow, turn right and follow it along to a stile into the next field. Walk up to the farm buildings and take the farm road between them and follow it to a gate that leads back into a field. In the field, follow the hedgeline on your left to the corner of the field. Cross a stile here, then walk across the field, heading slightly down the slope, to a stile onto Ewyas Harold Common.

5 Once over the stile, head across the common, staying above a bracken-covered area and disused quarry on your right, aiming for a gravelled track ahead. Turn left on the track and then right at the fork soon reached (or cut across the sward to join this other track). Follow this downhill, ignoring the turning to Hill Place off to the left, heading towards a stone-built house. Immediately this side of the house, take a metal gate into a field on the left, and walk along the hedgeline on your left. From here you get good views over Dore Abbey.

You will soon come to a field fenced to keep deer in, where a tall stepped structure leads you over the fence. Once in the 'deer field' keep walking on the same line that you followed along the side of the hill and in due course you will pick up a hedgeline to follow on your right. When this drops away to the right, keep ahead to another tall stepped structure by which to leave the field. Walk down the track from this field, the path bearing left through one gate at the side of the last farm building and across a small patch of grass to another gate out onto a road.

6 Turn right on the road, turning right at the first junction (thereby continuing straight ahead) and left at the second (and so almost straight ahead again). Cross the river Dore and walk past Abbey Dore Court on your right. Immediately past the complex of buildings that form part of Abbey Dore Court, turn right on a track which shortly turns to a footpath. This shadows high fencing on your left that delineates the edge of SAS training grounds. The path swings first right and then left, with glimpses of Abbey Dore Court's gardens to the right. The path will lead you over a footbridge across the

ABBEY DORE COURT GARDENS

The eight acres of gardens set around the Dore river feature collections of hellebores, paeonia, astrantia, ferns and bamboos, a 1-acre walled garden and an additional 4-acre meadow with unusual trees. In past years the gardens were open to the public, but they were permanently closed in 2021.

Dore into a field, on the far side of which is Dore Abbey. The path heads across the field, aiming for a point a bit to the left of the abbey. A series of gates will then lead you into the abbey grounds.

DORE ABBEY

As you near the abbey you will cross the line of the old mill leat which both served as the main drain and powered a mill that stood a few yards to the left. (To the right of the abbey, as you stand at this point, the leat had already served a larger corn mill.) You may also notice the traces of two rooflines on the end of the north transept which represent the position of the roof over the monks' dormitory, the roof clearly having been raised at some point. At ground level on the corner of the north transept you will see the remains of the chapter house.

The abbey was founded in 1147 by Robert I of Ewyas as a Cistercian monastery. The existing church was begun around 1180 and building work carried on for some 40 years. The property passed to John Scudamore at its dissolution in 1536. In 1633 the then Viscount Scudamore carried out extensive repairs to rescue the part of the structure that stands today as the parish church. He blocked off the nave and aisles (traces of the nave can still be seen outside the present building), re-roofed the remaining structure (the transepts, crossing, choir and retrochoir of the abbey) and built a tower over one of the south transept chapels. It gives the building a somewhat ungainly appearance; the space inside is pleasingly unusual and full of oddities. On the walls of the remaining transept and crossing are a number of 17th- and 18th-century wall paintings, including one of a skeleton representing Death leaning on his spade, another of Time with a scythe and hour-glass and several texts; a heavy 17th-century screen attributed to John Abel; two 13th-century effigies of knights; the tomb-chest of John Hoskins, who died in 1638; an eastern ambulatory filled with pieces of carved stonework from parts of the abbey that have been otherwise largely destroyed; and, if you look carefully around the ambulatory, traces of the medieval paintwork that would once have covered the walls.

361

7 Walk up the path to the lychgate, cross the road and go over the stile on the far side. Once in the field, head to its top left-hand corner, to cross another stile into another field. Cross this field towards a stile near a white-painted cottage. But don't cross this stile: the path you want turns right in front of it and follows the field boundary on your left up the hillside, exiting the field by a stile in the top left-hand corner, the path then following a little alleyway between hedges to emerge back onto the common.

8 To return to Ewyas Harold, having passed through the gate at the end of the alleyway, turn left. Before long you should spot a post with a yellow marker arrow. Follow this direction to take a wide grassy track, initially marked with Herefordshire Trail signs, keeping straight ahead when you meet other paths. The track will cross a small 'valley'. On the far side take the left-hand fork, which will lead you to a T-junction of tracks, where you turn left, and after a few yards meet a road that serves some of the houses on the common. Turn right and follow the road to a T-junction, where you turn left. This quickly leads to a further junction of tracks and roads near an information board which tells you about local wildlife and includes a map of the common. Take the track to the right (as you approached the board), passing below the gravel track that leads to houses on the edge of the common. This track will lead you to the right of a cream-painted house and then downhill to a stile. Cross the stile and follow the line of the old hedge through a field down the hillside, the path then bearing left alongside the boundary of a house to a stile into the next field. Head down this field to its far side, where a gate leads you out onto a road. Keep ahead and this road leads you back to the Temple Bar Inn.

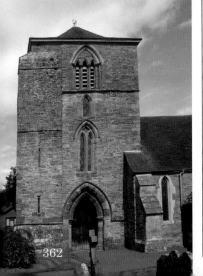

EWYAS HAROLD CHURCH
The church (shown in the photograph on the left) was granted to St Peter's Abbey in Gloucester (now the cathedral) early in the 12th century. The tower, with walls 7 feet thick, dates from the 13th century, and was probably used as a place of refuge.

Walk 52
Rowlestone & Walterstone

6 miles, largely on paths across fields or alongside field edges (many laid to pasture), some of them part of the Marches Way, minor roads and tracks. Several stiles. Includes two churches, a castle motte and a hillfort. In 2021 a footbridge was due to be repaired but there is an alternative track and shallow ford that can be used – you may want to do the walk in Wellingtons!

Park in the car park next to Rowlestone church (GR 374 273).

1 From the car park walk downhill with the church on your left to where the road bends to the left. Before it does so, turn right onto a track and immediately take the stile to its left. The path initially follows the line of the fence on your right (beyond which is a new bungalow). Keep following the fence as it curves to the right to then cross a small stream by a plank bridge. Then take the slightly sunken path downhill, keeping to the left of a group of trees, aiming to the left of a telegraph pole in the hedgeline where two lines of wires meet. Keep descending to reach a gateway which adjoins some woodland to its left. Continuing on much the same line the path then crosses the stream ahead by a footbridge.

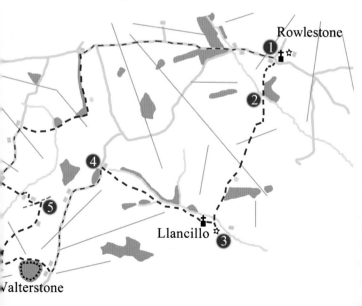

363

ROWLESTONE CHURCH AND CASTLE MOUND

Little is known of the castle: no traces of buildings have been found on the motte, whilst the 14th-century Court Farm probably stands on the site of any bailey that might have existed.

As for the church, the nave and chancel are Norman, with later windows inserted. The tower dates to the 13th or 14th century. The main interest is the work of the Herefordshire School (see p.221) on the south doorway and chancel arch. The capitals to the south doorway have carvings of birds similar to some of those on the Kilpeck doorway, but different in that they have a disc above their back, framed in the curve of the backward-looking head and spread of wing. The tympanum depicts Christ in Majesty or the Ascension and some similarities with earlier work in Hereford Cathedral suggest that the sculptor here, believed to be the 'chief master' of the school, received early training at the cathedral. The capitals to the chancel arch are carved with human figures and birds; as they are considered to be somewhat more restrained than the carvings on the doorway, they may have been by an assistant. The upside-down figures relate to St Peter, who was crucified upside-down by choice as he didn't wish to be compared with Christ, and the birds perhaps refer to Peter's hearing of the cock crowing on the Mount of Olives on the night that Jesus was betrayed.

Also of interest are the pair of 15th-century wrought-iron bracket candelabras on the north and south walls of the chancel, with six swans on the south bracket and six cocks on the north bracket, separated, in each case, by a fleur de lis.

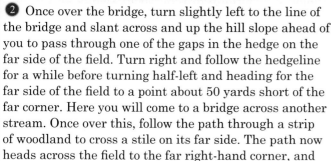

2 Once over the bridge, turn slightly left to the line of the bridge and slant across and up the hill slope ahead of you to pass through one of the gaps in the hedge on the far side of the field. Turn right and follow the hedgeline for a while before turning half-left and heading for the far side of the field to a point about 50 yards short of the far corner. Here you will come to a bridge across another stream. Once over this, follow the path through a strip of woodland to cross a stile on its far side. The path now heads across the field to the far right-hand corner, and

in so doing gradually closes in on the field boundary on your right – there may be a headland path left around the edge of the field which you may prefer to take. In the corner, pass through a gateway ahead of you into the field beyond and continue following field boundaries on your right. As you near the crest of the hill you will come to a stile well concealed in the hedgerow on your right. Cross this stile and then turn half-left, to pass just to the right of a small pond with its fringe of trees near the crest. On the horizon is the Sugarloaf, straight ahead of you. From

365

Keep the hillfort to your left, and follow it round, in due course bearing slightly left, just to the right of a group of trees, to the corner of the field, where there is a stile just below the hillfort. Cross this stile and follow the overgrown field boundary on your left downhill, after some 50 yards or so turning left onto a track which leads over another stile and slants downhill towards a farm. (If the path is very muddy, you may wish to cross into the neighbouring field.)

5 Cross the stile at the end and head down the track, but before you join the tarmac lane, take the second of three gates on the right, the path now following a hedge on your right along the hillside. Cross the field boundary at the far end of the field and keep following the hedge on your right. At the far end of this second field, you go through a footpath gate ahead. Diagonally cross this next field, aiming just to the left of the farm buildings on the far side. Here you go through two footpath gates separated by a plank bridge, then follow the farm's garden round to a gate onto a track. Turn left on the track and walk down to where it meets another track.

6 Turn left here, and then bear right down a concrete lane towards another house. Immediately past the stone barn on the right of this lane, go through the gate on the right of the lane and diagonally cross the little field to its far corner, entering the next field by another gate. Here turn left and follow the valley bottom till you are immediately between it and the house now on your left. Here you will find a bridge across the stream, which you take. Walk up the bank on the far side of the bridge, and keep heading up hill, in due course aiming for the far left-hand corner of the field, to the

Contents

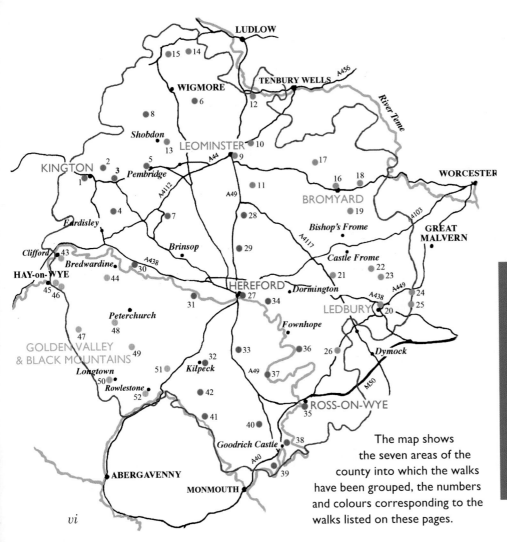

LUDLOW

15 14

WIGMORE

6

TENBURY WELLS

12

River Teme

A456

8

Shobdon

13

5

LEOMINSTER

10

9

A44

17

KINGTON

2

3

Pembridge

1

A4112

11

A49

16 18

BROMYARD

WORCESTER

4

7

19

28

Bishop's Frome

A4117

GREAT MALVERN

A4103

Eardisley

Brinsop

29

Castle Frome

Clifford 43

Bredwardine

A438

30

22

21

23

A449

24

44

HAY-ON-WYE

45 46

HEREFORD

27 34

Dormington

A438

25

20

LEDBURY

31

Fownhope

Peterchurch

48

36

26

Dymock

47

GOLDEN VALLEY & BLACK MOUNTAINS

49

33

Longtown

51

32

Kilpeck

A49

37

50

Rowlestone

52

42

M50

ROSS-ON-WYE

35

41

40

38

Goodrich Castle

A40

39

ABERGAVENNY

MONMOUTH

vi

The map shows
the seven areas of the
county into which the walks
have been grouped, the numbers
and colours corresponding to the
walks listed on these pages.

Key

— A road
— B road
— Other tarmacked road
▦ Woodland
— Stream or river
▪ Building or group of buildings
— Indication of slope from hill top
— Line of walk
— Other paths
① Point on the map relating to same point in walk description
🍺 Pub
☕ Tea Room

The key above is to accompany
the maps of the walk routes
throughout the book.

the county), and the historic features that the walk includes. It also indicates places en route which can be open to the public at certain times of the year or day, to give you a chance to plan in advance when to do the walk if you want to include such places. A further idea of the historic features of the walk can be gained by leafing through it and seeing what is included in the boxes of information. The walk descriptions will also often include a line or two about buildings or other features encountered. We have tried to give a reasonable depth of information about the places seen en route, but you may want to supplement it from other sources; excellent church guides are available in many churches, for example. All the photographs included with each walk have been taken on that walk (or on visits to buildings or gardens that can be included on the walk) – except one. Have fun working out which. (Clue: its subject can actually be seen from the walk but not so closely.)

Researching and writing the book has certainly been fun. It's (suitably) a coming full circle for Logaston Press, whose first publication (in 1985) was *Walks and More*. Since then – and it was originally intended to be Logaston's one and only book – more than 350 titles have been produced under the Logaston imprint, many of them covering the historical ground summarised briefly in the boxed information scattered throughout this book. We hope that the places it will help you to visit (many of them only accessible on foot) will provide you with a great deal of interest and pleasure. And if

the walking is too much, we hope the information and photographs will allow you to enjoy the landscape and history of this beautiful county in the bramble-free comfort of your own home.

We are very grateful to Heather Hurley, Paul Olver, Keith Ray, Ron Shoesmith, Alan Stoyel and Malcolm Thurlby for their help with historical research, and to our friends and family for submitting with such enthusiasm and good grace to joining us on some of the walks, braving all weathers, conditions and uncertainties, and patiently bearing with us during the necessary pauses to discuss the route, the view or the appropriate preposition. In particular, many thanks to Richard Johnson, John Rogers and Rafa Peñas, Peter Shackleton, Kathy Leong, Varasahaya and Shantipala, Satyalila, Heather, Austin, Will and Alfie Owens, David Styan, Susie, Ivor and Martin Dunkerton, and of course Meg (see p.73). In helping update the walks in 2021, we would like to thank the Wheeler household and Lokeshvara.

Andy & Karen Johnson
November 2021

1 Kington
& the black and white villages of north-west Herefordshire

KINGTON

Kington, recorded as Chingtune in the Domesday Book of 1086, probably derives its name from the Old English meaning 'King's town or manor', the king in question being the Harold who fell at Hastings. As Earl Harold Godwinson, he had been given the task of driving the Welsh back in the years after an attack on Hereford in 1055 which saw the city and cathedral ravaged. Many Saxons, however, must have dwelt peacefully alongside their Welsh neighbours, as several settlements with Saxon names are found in the Radnor Plain, to the west of Offa's Dyke. Nevertheless, much of the area was still recorded as 'waste' because of this fighting at the time of the Domesday Survey.

In 1108 Henry I granted the manor of Kington to Adam de Port, a grant which included five knights' fees scattered as afar afield as Dorset. The grant implied an intention to establish a major castle at Kington and probably a borough settlement. In 1173 a later Adam de Port rebelled against Henry II and was forced to flee to Scotland. By then the lordship had become combined with the office of sheriff of Herefordshire, an office that continued with the de Braoses, who were now granted the lordship. The castle was abandoned by 1230 after nearby Huntington had been made the centre of another lordship. Even so, Kington remained as the local centre for agricultural trade and struggled on, a refuge in times of trouble being provided by the church tower, which was at one time a separate structure from the church. The town must have been thriving in the early 1600s, for John Abel, the 'King's Carpenter' was commissioned to build both a new market hall and Lady Hawkins' School, which was opened in 1632. The current market hall, built of intense red brick, with a clock tower added later, is at the bottom of Church Street. Nearby is Kington Museum.

The canals never reached Kington, and the railways did so somewhat belatedly (and have since gone), but in the early 19th century the town was served by a horse-drawn tramway that linked lime and stone works at Burlingjobb and Dolyhir via the town to the coalfields of south Wales. This also furthered the establishment of the Kington Foundry, subsequently Meredith's at Sunset (confusingly on the east of the town), which employed about 120 people at its zenith.

Walk 1
Kington & Hergest

6.5 miles, largely on grassy tracks, forest tracks, some paths across fields and minor roads within Kington. A few stiles. Includes an arboretum famous for its rhododendrons (so especially good in May), the home of the Hound of the Baskervilles, a castle motte, an ancient racecourse, a stone with its own folklore, and a church. Check the opening times for Hergest Croft Gardens (see page 9).

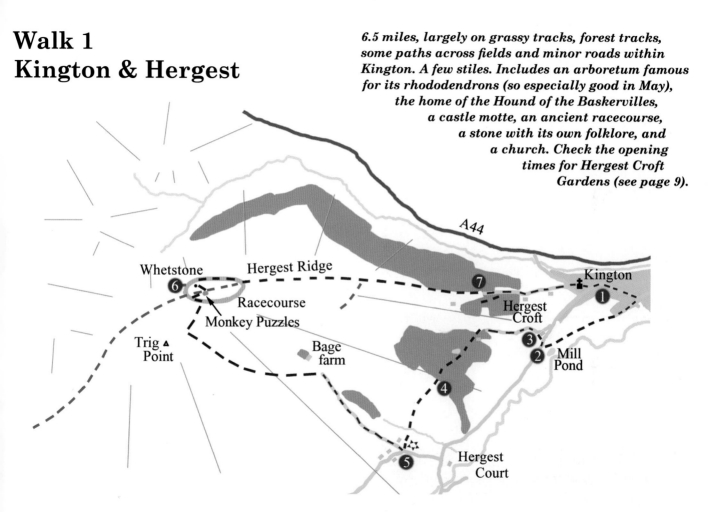

A44

Whetstone

Hergest Ridge

6

Kington

7

Racecourse

Monkey Puzzles

Hergest
Croft

1

Trig ▲
Point

Bage
farm

3

2

Mill
Pond

4

5

Hergest
Court

3

This walk starts from The Square near the Swan Inn (GR 295 567). There are parking spaces in the square or round the corner at the far end of the square from the Swan.

1 Walk down Church Street towards the centre of Kington, turning right at the bottom of the hill onto Mill Street, passing the market hall and then the museum. Continue along Mill Street, which becomes Park Road, and go through the gates just past Sargents bus depot on the left to enter the Recreation Ground. Follow the tarmacked path to its end in front of a house, go through the kissing gate on the right and then keep to the left of the line of large trees to cross to a kissing gate to enter a field. Follow the path across the field to another kissing gate, then continue on the path past a mill-pond to join a road.

2 Turn right on the road, and after 100 yards or so cross a stile into a field on the left. Follow the line of hedge on your right uphill, and the path will then pass around a cottage on your right to join a lane.

3 Turn left on the lane and it will bring you into a field in a narrow valley. Ignore signs for paths off to your right and keep on the lane to a cattle grid and gate near a stream into a block of woodland. Keep following the track in the woodland. This is a public path, but further on, off to each side are private paths which are part of Hergest Croft Gardens. If you wish to explore these, please put some money in the box you'll soon come to on the right opposite a house on the left.

Keep on the track, which will pass through immense rhododendron groves, past a shady pool and then rise up the hillside beyond to leave the wood via a kissing gate.

4 Here the path crosses the field to the far side, on a line that rises gently uphill, passing through a gate into the field beyond. At this point the path follows the hedge on your right, going through more gates as it slopes downhill to enter some scrub below the huge motte of a Norman castle. Look across the valley on your left to spy out the partly timber-framed and partly stone-built Hergest Court.

Cross the stream in the dip, then go up the slope on the opposite side, following the fence

HERGEST COURT

This house must have been commenced in the late 1260s as one timber has been dated by dendrochronology as having been felled in 1267 and some floorboards dated to 1307. There is a record of a visit to the house by Bishop Swinfield of Hereford in 1290. A stone outbuilding to the south of the present building has been dated to *c.*1320 and is thought to be the remnant of the solar block of a former great hall. The Vaughans acquired the site some time after 1400 and began a rebuild in about 1430, perhaps due to damage caused in the wars with Owain Glyndwr. The Welsh bard Lewis Glyn Cothi described the court as having eight strong buildings, but these were demolished during the 18th century. The court was once home to Thomas and Ellen Vaughan, whose tomb can be seen in Kington church. Thomas Vaughan's spirit is said to have troubled the area down the centuries, tormenting animals and people alike to the extent that the trade at Kington market was affected. This led the townsfolk to arrange for 12 parsons with 12 candles to assemble in the church, together with a woman with a new-born baby, to tempt the spirit into the building and then try to 'read' it down into a silver snuff box. When Vaughan's spirit appeared, it overcame all the parsons save one who managed the deed; the snuff box was then buried in the bottom of Hergest Pool, by the house, and a large stone placed on top. When this pool was recently drained, bubbles appeared from the bottom and such was the concern amongst the workforce that they might be allowing Vaughan's spirit back into the world that work was halted for a while. The spirit of Vaughan's large black dog is felt to have given Arthur Conan Doyle the idea for his *Hound of the Baskervilles*, the local theory being that the story was set on Dartmoor to protect Hergest Court and the local Baskerville family from association with the plot. Of more reliable folklore, here was found the *Red Book of Hergest*, from which the *Mabinogion* was compiled.

on your right to a gate in the far right-hand corner of this patch of ground, though you may first wish to climb the castle mound. Go through the gate and turn left to immediately reach a crossroads of tracks and tarmacked lanes.

5 Turn right at this 'crossroads' to walk uphill, the lane in due course leading over a cattle grid onto Hergest Ridge. Turn half-left to follow a grassy track alongside a gully. This will lead you up to near the crest of the hill but before doing so, at the end of the part of the hillside that is thickly covered with bracken, you meet another track on which you turn right. Turn left when you soon meet a broad green sward, once the track for Kington racecourse. From 1825 the racecourse hosted regular events until around 1880. It replaced an earlier course around the top of Bradnor Hill (the hill to the north-east of where you're standing), which began use in about 1770. Follow the line of the racecourse for a short way, before branching off to the right to head for a group of monkey puzzles.

Here you have views over to Radnor Forest to the north, and, to the right and on a clear day, the Long Mynd, and swivelling round further, the Clee Hills, the Malverns, May Hill and the Black Mountains to the south-west.

From the monkey puzzles, head left and slightly back on yourself from the direction you approached them to reach, amongst the gorse and before you reach the course of the circular racecourse, the Whetstone.

HERGEST CASTLE TWTS

This prominent castle mound is probably the result of artificially steepening an existing knoll. There is a small motte towards the west which may hold the remains of a stone tower. It is possible that the castle was never completed. The last occupant of the site is thought to have been Hwyel ap Meurig, hereditary reeve of Gladestry. It was he who began the building of Hergest Court (see p.5). The family assumed the anglicised name of Clanvow(e) in the 13th century and long predated the Vaughans, who arrived after 1400.

WALTERSTONE HILLFORT

The roughly circular hillfort covers an area of some 9¾ acres and comprises three ramparts (now not as high than they once were) separated by two ditches, the outer one of which may have contained water. The original entrance was probably at the north-north-east. The camp has been dug over and planted with flowers and shrubs, but it is said that in the process of digging nothing was found but some Elizabethan pottery.

left of a house. Pass out of the field by the stile here and onto the lane beyond.

7 Turn right on the lane. You can now simply follow this lane back to the church if you wish, by staying on it and ignoring all turnings to right or left. However, if you want to do part of the remainder of the walk on paths, follow the lane past a track to a farm on the left where there is also a house close to the roadside and keep going till you approach a part stone, part painted cottage ('Fair View') on the left. Just before you reach this cottage you will see a stile (possibly overgrown) into a field on the right. Cross this and then follow the hedge on your left to a gate at the far end of the field. Pass through this and then bear slightly left and cross this next field to find a bridge across the stream ahead. (To find the bridge, keep some 40 yards to the right of a group of tall trees beyond a heap of stone slabs at the bottom of the field.) Once over the bridge, climb the steps on the far side and then bear half-left up the bank and through a small piece of woodland to enter the next field by a gate. Once in this field, follow the hedge on your left, leaving the field at the far end by a small gate to enter some young woodland beyond. Head to the right-hand edge of the woodland, and follow it along, turning left at the end on a path into the woodland and then right after a few yards to cross a stile. Once over this turn left. Cross five field boundaries, all in the corners of fields, as you keep following the field boundaries on your left back to the lane. Turn right once on the lane and follow this back to the church.

Index